THE HYPERLOCAL, HYPERFAST REAL ESTATE AGENT

How to Dominate Your Real Estate Market in Under a Year—I Did It and So Can You!

DANIEL JAMES LESNIAK
BROKER AND MBA

To hear interviews with some of the top real estate agents, marketers, trainers, and coaches in the world, check out the HyperFast Agent Podcast!

We dig deep into real estate, marketing, motivation, and more to get valuable insights from the brightest minds in the business. Visit hyperfastpodcast.com to tune in OR search your favorite podcast platform for HyperFast Agent.

Want to see the reports we use to generate buyer and seller top-of-funnel leads? Go to hyperfastdownloads.com to get your exclusive free download!

The HyperLocal, HyperFast Real Estate Agent
Copyright © 2017 Daniel James Lesniak

Library of Congress Control Number: 2017932258
ISBN: 978-0998354507
Published by DKB Publishing, Arlington, VA
Printed in the United States of America

Disclaimer: Daniel James Lesniak is a licensed real estate broker in DC, MD, and VA with Optime Realty, also doing business as the Orange Line Living (livetheorangeline.com) and Keri Shull (kerishull.com) teams.

Table of Contents

About the Author i

Praise for the Book ii

Client Testimonials iv

Prologue.. 1

Chapter 1: Finding Sellers with Under-Door Notes........................... 11

Chapter 2: Positioning Through Targeted E-mail Newsletters 25

Chapter 3: Leveraging Bidding Wars and Open Houses 45

Chapter 4: Using People to Find Buyers 60

Chapter 5: Finding Craigslist Buyers—Competing for Listings......... 67

Chapter 6: Open Houses: Finding Buyers and Selling Listings.......... 89

Chapter 7: Buying Your Own Listings 105

Chapter 8: Pre-Selling to Other Agents... 118

Chapter 9: Using Signs and Finding Inventory on Craigslist 125

Chapter 10: Opening More Doors Through Seller Financing.......... 133

Chapter 11: Getting Buyers to Beat Other Buyers to Listings.......... 138

Chapter 12: Getting the Best Deals in New Construction 144

Chapter 13: Concluding Thoughts.. 149

Epilogue.. 154

100 Tips and Strategies 156

Index... 175

Join Our Team... 181

Learn About Coaching 183

Referral Network for Agents 185

Looking to Buy or Sell?... 187

About the Author

Daniel James Lesniak began his career in real estate in 2012 after having successful careers both as a naval submarine officer and a defense contractor. His hyperlocal strategy led to one of the fastest starts in real estate, with over $22 million in sales in his first year. Since 2012 Dan has gone on to create the Orange Line Living Team, which later merged with the Keri Shull Team.

In 2014 the team was ranked fourth in the world at Keller Williams. In 2015 the team became part of Optime Realty, a brokerage co-founded by Dan and his wife, Keri. Since then the team has gone on to become one of the top 33 teams in the nation and number one in Virginia, as ranked by Real Trends in the *Wall Street Journal*.

Dan and Keri are also real estate developers and investors and have directly developed over $15 million in real estate. Dan has a Bachelor of Science degree from the United States Naval Academy, a Master of Arts from the University of Maryland, and a Master of Business Administration from Georgetown University. He is an avid endurance athlete, having completed 13 marathons (including three Boston Marathons) and five Ironman challenges. Dan lives in Arlington, VA, with his wife Keri; their sons Braden and Grayson; and their daughter Kierra.

Praise for the Book

I have been coaching realtors for 22 years. Dan is the best businessman who sells real estate that I've ever seen. He has great systems, structures, and processes. That is what separates him from the rest!

Rick Ruby - Core Head Coach

One of my favorite sayings is "follow the yellow brick road." In this book, Dan clearly lays out the path to the Emerald City, avoiding all the dangers of creating your own way. In Dan's first year, he closed over $22 million in sales, a feat matched by only the tiniest fraction of real estate agents—regardless of experience. If you are looking for a step-by-step plan from someone who has done it, this is the book for you!

Pam O'Bryant, Chief Engagement Officer for
Keller Williams Capital Properties, Contributor to Gary Keller's
The Millionaire Real Estate Agent *book*

There is no greater opportunity right now in the real estate industry than there is in the expansion market. This will require you to grow in your existing market and know how to expand in new ones. This book is a great example of how to rapidly expand in any market and is a must read for expansion team leaders.

Noah Ostroff, Chief Executive Officer of
Global Living and
Top-Selling Keller Williams Agent

Dan Lesniak is the real deal. He runs the most profitable real estate team I know of, hands down. If you want to compress time to achieve your goals, listen to this guy and take action now!

Jeff Latham, President of Latham Realty Unlimited
with 275 homes sold annually

Dan and I first met when he was just getting started in the business, and I have been blown away at how he was able to grow his brand so rapidly in a very competitive market. Dan's creative approach and tenacity has served him well, and he is a great example of how to commit and succeed as a young real estate agent.

Thad Wise, Senior Vice President with First Savings Mortgage Corporation
and $100 Million Loan Officer

Dan Lesniak is by far one of the brightest and highest-skilled real estate agents I have had the pleasure of working with; his strategies for his clients are brilliant! Dan has succeeded in one of the most competitive markets in the country, while also growing his brokerage and giving back to the community.

Elysia Stobbe, Real Estate RockStar and #1 Best Selling Author of
How to Get Approved for the Best Mortgage
Without Sticking a Fork in Your Eye
(*ElysiaStobbeBooks.com*
youtube.com/c/ElysiaStobbeMortgage
info@bestmortgagebook.com)

Client Testimonials

When I was first thinking about selling my home, I did not think I was going to use a listing agent. Due to the high demand in Clarendon Park and a recent bidding war on my neighbor's home, I felt confident that a listing agent was not necessary.

When Dan Lesniak first contacted me, his message was that his marketing strategy would get my home seen at its very best by the largest number of potential buyers, which would create competition among buyers to get me the best offer. I was not sure at first that it would net me more money, but I decided to give him a try and I credit that decision for making me over $50,000.

His team helped me throughout the entire process, including selecting and managing painters and staging professionals who could work around my family's busy schedule to get the house in the best possible shape, creating the best print and online marketing materials, promoting and managing an open house weekend with over 100 groups of buyers, directing an offer process and negotiating strategy, tapping the networks of other top agents, and more. As a result of his unique marketing and superior negotiating strategies, I accepted an offer with no contingencies that was nearly seven percent above list price and $53,000 higher than the previous sold unit, which had only closed the week before. If you are thinking about selling your home, I could recommend no one better than Dan and the Orange Line Living Team.

Arlington, VA, Seller (Clarendon Park Townhomes)

No one knows the Arlington, VA, area as well as Dan Lesniak. My wife and I were passively looking, and he found us a great deal in a new condo building in the area. He has the connections and insight to find deals that aren't being advertised and the persistence to stay in touch with buyers to find the right deal. If you are looking for a place in the Arlington area, I highly recommend working with Dan to find you a great deal, even if you are just initiating the buying process.

Arlington, VA, Buyer (Gaslight Square Condo)

Dan helped me buy my first condo in a very competitive market. He was really helpful and responsive. He also has excellent knowledge of the real estate market in the DC area. I highly recommend Dan Lesniak if you are looking for a real estate agent.

Arlington, VA, Buyer (Station Square Condo)

I used Dan Lesniak to buy my first home. He helped me through the entire process. I highly recommend him to help you buy or sell your home. He will get the job done.

Arlington, VA, Buyer (Lexington Square Condo)

Dan and his colleagues provided us with the best experience we ever had in selling our condo. He came in, gave us a price, and actually within just a few days sold our place for above the asking price! He was professional and took care of everything, which made it easy for us. When we had questions, he and his team were always responsive in a timely manner. Would highly recommend them.

Arlington, VA, Seller (Continental Condo)

Dan Lesniak is very thorough in his approach to selling and buying real estate. He was always making sure to think of all avenues for selling my home and reminded me of options that I had not considered. He was always good with the open house showings, and very good at coordinating all the people who wanted to see the unit. Highly recommended if you are looking for quality results within a short time frame.

Washington, DC, Seller (Penn Quarter)

Dan Lesniak helped me sell two houses (both at record prices) and buy another. I couldn't be happier. Dan's team was responsive, professional and honest. I would highly recommend him to anyone buying/selling in Northern VA.

Arlington, VA, Buyer and Seller (Phoenix Condo and Waverly Hills)

Dan is a great real estate agent, and it was a pleasure to work with him. His MBA degree is a qualification that initially caught my attention and in working with him—I think this does put him at an advantage. I was also impressed by his marketing technique and his style—which is not pushy but informative. I value responsibility and reliability, and I found Dan to be exceptional in both of these qualities, and I think he worked very hard towards a successful listing and quick and efficient sale of my condo. I recommend Dan Lesniak strongly to anyone looking for a competent realtor who can deliver results. I wish him all the best.

Arlington, VA, Seller (Westview Condo)

We had a fantastic experience working with Dan Lesniak. He is the consummate real estate professional. He represented us in both selling our condo and purchasing a new home. His deep knowledge of the local real estate market and superb negotiating skills were essential in helping us get top dollar in selling our condo. Additionally, Dan was able to leverage his extensive personal network to help us purchase our new home before it even came on the market. Dan is always quick to return calls and takes the extra time to make sure that every aspect of the sales process is proceeding in his client's best interest. It was a pleasure working with him. I have already recommended Dan to friends and will be excited to work with him again in the future.

Arlington, VA, Buyer and Seller
(Clarendon 3131 Condo and Clarendon Park Townhomes)

Dan Lesniak is a real estate agent extraordinaire. He manages to be both professional and approachable at the same time. He works diligently to get the sales transaction completed whether he is representing the buyer and/or the seller. (In our case, he represented the seller but assisted us as the purchasers in the transaction. Then Dan listed our newly purchased condo for rent and found us a tenant within a week!) He is honest and trustworthy and best of all, he keeps in touch and returns calls and emails promptly. Would recommend Dan without hesitation!

Arlington, VA, Buyer (Phoenix Condo)

I had an excellent experience with Dan Lesniak. Experience tells me that I can trust Dan's advice, that he acts in his client's best interest, that he's extremely proactive, and that he has an excellent professional network. In short—I will not hesitate to ask for his assistance the next time I need a realtor. Dan not only helped me through my purchase of a short sale property in Alexandria, he also rented out my condo in Clarendon. The short sale in Alexandria went smoothly: Dan guided me through the process, providing expert advice that informed me of what I could expect at each step. With respect to the rental: Dan leveraged his extensive network to find an excellent tenant, complete with a security deposit, literally just ONE DAY after he started showing the place.

Arlington and Alexandria, VA, Buyer and Seller (Clarendon 1021)

Dan Lesniak is a consummate professional who has an expert knowledge of the greater Arlington area. Regardless of time of day, Dan promptly responds to all inquiries and helped us prepare our house for sale. I highly recommend Dan and will seek out his help in finding our future home.

Arlington, VA, Seller (Phoenix Condo)

My experience working with Dan Lesniak was extremely positive. He is very knowledgeable of the local market (i.e., he knew all the condo buildings in the area and immediately let me know when comparables went on the market), very responsive, and hardworking. He is eager to help and went out of his way to help make the process easier for me (i.e., he helped me stage my condo to make it look more presentable). Most importantly, he has the wherewithal and moxie to get the job done. I highly recommend Dan!

Arlington, VA, Seller (Phoenix Condo)

I had an extremely positive experience working with Dan Lesniak. Having worked with multiple agents in the past, Dan clearly separated himself from others in the level of service and professionalism. I think his experience and education is likely more broad and comprehensive than most agents, and this comes through in organizational skills and process management. I have already recommended Dan to others and will continue to do so.

Arlington/Alexandria, VA, Buyer and Seller
(Phoenix Condo and Cameron Station)

Dan Lesniak truly exceeded my expectations in terms of his knowledge, skill, and dedication in assisting me to find a home. As a first-time home buyer I was new to the process – Dan certainly eased any fears and helped to facilitate the process step-by-step – finding a home, financing, negotiating, etc... What really made him stick out in my mind was his availability; I had no reservations about calling /texting/emailing Dan anytime a question popped into my head (this happened frequently and often at inconvenient times)–not once can I say I waited longer than about 30 minutes to get response– this includes an email I sent at 1:15 a.m. I don't know when this guy sleeps. What I do know is that I would recommend him without reservation!

Arlington, VA, Buyer (Rhodes Hill Square)

Dan Lesniak managed the entire process of my recent move with a high level of expertise and professionalism. His local market knowledge was exceptional, and he routinely made sure I was one of the first buyers to see properties when they came on the market. He had an expert level of knowledge on financing and helped me choose the mortgage that best fit my needs. After I moved into my new home, he knew the right contractors to get work done on my new place. Throughout the entire process Dan was able to help me understand all of my options and saved me money throughout every step. I would definitely recommend him to anyone.

Arlington, VA, Buyer (Phoenix Condo)

Acknowledgments

There are so many people that have helped me—up to my real estate career and since—that I would like to thank.

My first mentor in real estate was Pam O'Bryant. Although I self-started my career at Century 21 Redwood Realty, Pam gave me instrumental advice throughout that first year even thought I had not yet joined her company. Thank you for recruiting me and for your persistence during the year it took for me to make the move. I am grateful for the training and advice you gave me before, during, and after my time at Keller Williams, which played a huge role in my growing from a solo-agent model to a team.

I am so lucky to have such wonderful parents, James Lesniak and Rhonda Goodman. Thank you for all of your support and for being people I could learn from. Mom, I especially thank you for your support on my book and for your substantive and thoughtful commentary along the way.

Throughout the years I have learned from watching and interacting with real estate agents both in my market and across the country. There are far too many to thank individually, but you have all been people that have taught me so much.

As I grew from a solo agent to a team leader and broker I have been blessed to have had so many great people to work with along the way. You are all like family to me.

None of this would have been possible without all of my clients. I am so grateful for each and every one of you. I know buying or selling a home can be stressful and emotional, and one of the largest financial decisions in your life. Thank you for trusting me to help you.

I would also like to thank my editor, Bonnie Granat. Your support and technical expertise were critical in not only making this book the best it could be but in getting it across the finish line.

Finally, I would like to thank Keri, my wife and business partner. I have learned so much from you. You are an amazing woman in all of the roles you play: business leader, friend, mother, and wife. I have learned so much from you, specifically in the areas of interpersonal communication, vision, leadership, and personal development. Your optimism and love are an example for us all.

Foreword

As I was approaching my tenth year in the real estate industry in 2012, I reflected on changes in my life since graduating from Penn State University and moving to the Washington, DC, area. I had gone from a fresh college graduate selling single-family homes for a large builder during the crazy build-up in the early 2000s, to selling new condos, to becoming a general real estate agent, and to finally creating and growing my own real estate team. It was during that time I also decided I was ready to get married when I found the right guy.

Early in 2012, I began noticing postcards from some new real estate agent who called his business Orange Line Living. I lived in a town-home community very close to the Clarendon Metro, a very popular area on the Orange Line Metro in Arlington, VA, two miles outside of Washington, DC. New agents were always trying to break into the market, but agents who had been in the area for years if not decades typically dominated it. It was not uncommon to get a marketing piece from someone new. Lots of people tried, and they all failed. At first I thought, "Wow, he looks fairly young and new to the industry. I bet it will not be too long before he quits sending these!" Over the years I noticed most agents stop marketing efforts if they do not get immediate results. The winners realize it takes consistency over time.

To my surprise I kept seeing Orange Line Living cards in my mailbox, sometimes multiple ones in the same week. I also began to notice open house and for-sale directional signs with the Orange Line Living logo. Pretty soon this newbie seemed to be everywhere.

I first saw Dan in January of 2013 when he joined the Keller Williams office where I hung my licenses. At the first office-wide meeting our broker introduced Dan and his new Orange Line Living Team. I was surprised he had grown from beyond a single agent to a team. I was even more surprised when the broker said his team was going to give my team a run for its money. I never would have expected that coming from a person who at that point had been in the industry for barely a year.

It did not take me long to learn that my broker was not joking. Dan brought several new listings to the office, and all of them were in high-demand areas. They were the kind of listings that took agents years to get, and here was this new guy who had several of them all at the same time. When I researched his statistics I was shocked when I found out he sold over $20 million in his first year and almost all of his sales were in a three-block radius. I have been involved in real estate coaching programs for years, including Craig Proctor Coaching and the Core Training Program. I have also met top real estate agents at Tony Robbins seminars. I have always tried to surround myself with top real estate agents so I could learn and improve my business. I have yet to find another real estate agent who had a first-year success as high as Dan did or an agent who dominated an area to the extent Dan did.

Dan and I met soon after we saw each other at that initial team meeting. It turns out he was starting a title company and wanted to recruit me to use it. We instantly became great friends and soon thereafter began dating. Later that year we got engaged, and the following year we got married. Dan soon merged his team, The Orange Line Living Team, with my team, The Keri Shull Team.

The strategies and techniques Dan used to grow his business so quickly continue to work today for our team as it has grown to a team of over 30 people who sell nearly 400 homes a year. Since 2013 we have been the highest-selling team in Arlington, VA, and in 2015 we sold more volume than any other team in Virginia. Dan used his Navy and business-school background to apply a framework to real estate that I had not seen before in the business. His methods for how to look at a market, pick a segment, and target that segment are a proven model for success. If you are a new agent starting out, his methods will help you grow your business fast and lead to long-term success so that you don't become a part of the majority of agents who never make it anywhere in the business. If you are a veteran agent, his model will help you grow more market share in places where you already do business or help you expand to new areas. No matter where you are in your real estate agent career, this story is one that can be an example for you!

Keri Shull

Prologue

Prior to 2011 I did not envision having a career in real estate. Throughout my time in school and in the Navy I saw myself becoming a strategic consultant or part of a management team for a large corporation. After I finished my MBA at Georgetown University in 2010 I applied to several dozen companies. Like most MBA graduates I was looking forward to a big salary increase, in my case hopefully in the management consulting industry with one of the top companies. I had an undergraduate degree from the US Naval Academy and Masters degrees from the University of Maryland and Georgetown. In my career in the Navy I served aboard a nuclear missile submarine and worked at the Pentagon. In 2007 I began the evening MBA program at Georgetown University. When I completed the program in 2010 I was working as a defense contractor and was certain that with my background I would have no problem getting a job with one of the top-tier management consulting companies. After applying to several dozen companies, I got interviews from about a dozen or so. Most of them had between four and six interviews, so in total I did nearly 60 interviews.

Some of the companies gave me one round of interviews. Some of them gave me three or four rounds. The one thing they all had in common was that none of them offered me a job. I was shocked and almost in disbelief every time I got a rejection letter. When I made it through three rounds of interviews with McKinsey and Company and came up without an offer, I asked one of the senior level partners who interviewed me for some specific feedback. He told me that the partners did not think I had the ability to sell to clients and that while technical skills were important, they were looking for someone with more sales acumen.

While my interviews were going on, I was also in the process of buying a condo in the Arlington, VA, area. It was the second time I was purchasing a home in that area, and the fifth time overall. Being in the Navy, I took full advantage of the VA loan program and purchased my first home at the age of 23. By the time I was 25, I had already purchased three homes. I had also sold one of those homes and been a landlord previously. In 2011, when I was buying my fifth home, I decided to get my real estate license. I realized throughout the process that I did the majority of the searching for homes, analyzing loan options, and negotiating—activities normally done by real estate agents. During the transaction I realized there was a better way to do business than what I was experiencing. I did not imagine at that point that I would make it a career. I thought that if I got my license I would be able to save money while buying real estate and work on developing the sales skills that some of the world's "best" talent identifiers had said I was lacking. At first, I really did not think it would be something I would do as a full-time career.

Although many people have the perception that real estate agents live a large and glamorous life, the numbers paint a different picture. In 2012, the median gross income of those using the trademarked term REALTOR® to describe themselves (individuals who are members of the National Association of Realtors) was $43,500. For those with less than two years of experience, the median gross income was $9,700. This was according to a National Association of Realtors survey published in 2013. In that same year, the US poverty level guideline was $11,170. That means that typical real estate agents starting out could expect to make nearly $2,000 less than the poverty level in the United States for the first two years of their career. These figures are also the gross income levels, so these numbers do not take into account expenses real estate agents have to pay. Typical expenses include self-employment taxes, broker fees, association dues, lockbox fees, licensing and education fees, multiple listing fees, and vehicle expenses. These basic expenses do not even include any marketing expenses. So even if a Realtor spent nothing on marketing, the typical Realtor with less than two years' experience would make a net income of about half of the poverty level in the United States and the typical Realtor with 13 years of experience might earn a net income of just under the US median income level. Some reports indicate that more than 75% of people getting into the industry will last under two years. After looking at these numbers, it is hard to understand why there are over a million Realtors in the United States.

When I got my real estate license, I still had the job in the defense contracting industry that paid about $100,000 a year. So if I had looked too closely at the incomes made by most real estate agents, I could have expected to take a pay cut of over 50%. Furthermore, the chances of making more than my current salary did not seem likely. During that year, less than 20% of all Realtors made over $100,000 in gross commission. The chances of major success were even smaller. Less than 2% of all Realtors made over $250,000 in gross commission. Nearly everyone in the industry at this level had been in the industry for over ten years, had hundreds of past clients, and had great name recognition throughout the area where they sold.

This same market trend existed in the Greater DC area and in Arlington, VA, where I lived at the time. The average agent did about six transactions a year in the area. Less than 10% of real estate agents in the area did over 12 transactions a year. The bigger agents, who did more than 20 transactions a year, had several years or decades of experience. So my local market looked even harder to crack than the national averages.

The shortage of housing inventory for sale did not make the prospects of breaking into the market look any easier. In 2012, the Greater Washington, DC, area real estate market did not have a lot of inventory. This was even truer in the Arlington, VA, market, especially along the Orange Line Metro corridor, where I had lived for several years.

Despite the less than ideal outlook for new real estate agents, especially considering my current job status, I decided to make the jump into real estate and to establish a local real estate brand called Orange Line Living. I had immediate and unheard of success. I shattered the industry trends and almost instantly became the biggest agent in the market I went after, passing top agents who had decades of experience. In my first year as a full-time real estate agent, I had 37 transaction sides, which was about six times what the average agent in my area did. I sold over $22 million in total volume, which resulted in over

$500,000 of gross commission income. In recent years, large national real estate firms such as Keller Williams and Long and Foster have given rookie-of-the-year awards to agents who sold less than half that amount in their first year. I have yet to come across or hear about anyone who sold this much volume in his or her first year in real estate.[1]

In my first full year in real estate I became the top agent at my Century 21 Redwood Realty office, something that no other rookie sales agent has done since. Many companies recruit new agents by promising them leads, boasting about their "proprietary" technology systems, or touting their training programs. Although I was the top agent at my office from the beginning to the end of the year, not one of my clients came from a company-generated lead, nor can I look back and say that any company training or technology helped me get or close a client. The large-scale broker model does not have much to offer new agents. It is pretty much a "you are on your own" environment. Whether you are a new agent looking to start your career or an established agent looking to grow, you are going to have to figure out how to increase your leads and provide value to your clients.

Very few real estate agents generate a substantial amount of sales and commission, and of the few who do, most do not keep any of the money. So if generating sales is the first problem of most agents, remaining profitable is a close second. There are many possible reasons for this, but the primary one is that most real estate agents do not think like business owners and do not track revenues and expenses in order to analyze what spending leads to the most efficient business generation and how to maximize spending and time to get the best results for clients. This poor money and time management often leads to more stress for the typical high-volume real estate agent. I had a 70% profit margin, resulting in an income of over $350,000. Many large agents and teams operate at profit margins of less than 20%, so I had immediate success not only at generating a ton of sales but also at keeping the money from those sales. As a result, I still had a balanced life while producing at a high level, which translated into success for my clients.

---

[1] The exception to this would be agents who operate in a rebate-type model, such as Redfin, where the majority of the commission is rebated back to the client and not collected.

In my first year I quickly jumped into the top 1% of all agents in terms of not only sales but also net profit, which is often overlooked by those in the industry. In doing so I surpassed agents in my area who had decades of experience in the local market. Most importantly, I did all of this while providing extreme value to my clients, a key to ensuring long-term success.

My strategy worked not only in the short term but also over a longer period of time. In the five years since my initial year in real estate, Orange Line Living (livetheorangeline.com) grew from a brand operated in a solo-agent model, where I did everything, to a full-scale real estate team. During that time I met my wife, Keri Shull, who operated the Keri Shull Real Estate Team (kerishull.com). We ended up combining our teams and starting our own brokerage, Optime Realty. It has now grown to over 30 team members, and in 2015 we helped 370 families buy or sell homes, selling over $225 million in volume. That made us the highest-selling team in Virginia and one of the top 50 selling teams in the United States. Keri and I have successfully created systems that now help our agents and team members have success not seen in this industry. Our agents at the Orange Line Living and Keri Shull Teams averaged over $120,000 a year in net income. This number is nearly four times higher than the industry average for full-time agents. Most of our agents do this with less than two years of experience. The typical agent making over $100,000 in the overall industry has over a decade of experience. While jump-starting my business was very rewarding, Keri and I have gotten even more joy out of helping others do the same. Every year we bring on new people, most with zero industry experience, plug them into our system and watch them grow into top agents in a year or less.

I am excited to now have the opportunity to help even more people in the real estate industry. This book will specifically focus on my first year in real estate. I decided to share my story of how I made this transition because I think what I did is something anyone can do and because I would have appreciated learning from someone before I made this life-changing transition. This book will not offer a plug-and-play formula for instant success or a magical marketing system that will work in any market.

Instead, it will take you through the thought process of how I developed my overall strategy of applying the STP framework (segmenting, targeting, and positioning) and will look closely at the majority of the key transactions during my first year in real estate. For each transaction[2], I will discuss how I (1) developed the lead, (2) positioned myself as being the person best able to help them, and (3) closed the sale in a way that benefited everyone involved, but especially my clients. I think the best way to learn from this book is to use the stories to learn principles and ways of thinking and then determine how you can apply them to your own business and market in a way that will expand your business. I believe this collection of stories can help anyone—from agents who are just starting out to agents with decades-long experience and from solo agents to agents who have built large teams or brokerages. If you are just starting out, this book will help you think of successful ways to break into the market. If you are an experienced agent, this book will help you get more market share or think of ways to break into a new market.

Although there are many people who sell "instant success formulas" in real estate, I don't believe such approaches work. If they did, then the people selling such formulas would simply hire low-skilled workers to implement them in many markets. No one has ever had success doing that in the real estate industry. What works in one market may completely fail in another. However, I do believe that principles and strategies can have success in many different markets if they are applied in the right way at the right time. The more strategies you learn and the more strategic situations you think through, the greater your chance of successfully applying the right strategy at the right time will be. No matter what stage of your career, I believe this book will give you a better chance of applying the right strategy at the right time and having your business grow exponentially—like mine did—and in a way that creates maximum value for those around you.

---

[2] When discussing the transactions in this book, I changed the names of the people involved and slightly changed the price points in order to protect the privacy of those involved.

THE STP FRAMEWORK

When I decided to get my real estate license, I made the decision to focus on the geographical area where I lived. This was a conscious decision I made by applying the STP principle I learned in business-school marketing classes. That is, Segmentation, Targeting, and Positioning. I believe this approach can help any new agent break into the market with explosive growth and help established agents break into a new market and expand their business. If done properly, this growth will occur hyperfast. Most agents, I believe, do not have a systematic way of consciously determining where to focus their efforts. By failing to do that they rob themselves of the benefit of acting with intention. The following process will ensure that your efforts are directed and intentional, a key to producing results.

The first step is to segment the market. There are many ways to segment the real estate market. It can be done geographically, by occupation, by income level, or by your own sphere of influence. These are just a few of many examples. I decided to segment my market by geographical area. It is critical when going through the process of segmentation that you break the segments into sizes that are appropriate for your situation. Smaller segments are easier to take over. You can concentrate more resources in a smaller area. Larger segments are harder to take over but offer a bigger reward. If you are starting out, you will want to create smaller segments so that you can have a larger impact per segment. If you are an established agent with plenty of resources (size, experience, reputation, marketing budget, personnel, etc.), it might be appropriate for you to create bigger segments. The more competitive a market is, the harder it will be to take over a segment and vice versa.

In my case, I decided to segment the market based on geography. I think this is one of the more common ways to do it, but it often does not work for agents because they make their segments too big. The basis for my segmenting process was the Washington Metropolitan Area Transit Authority (the Metro) in the Greater Washington, DC, area. It consists of several different lines spanning the District of Columbia, Maryland, and Virginia. The Metro system plays a critical role in how communities are organized in the area, so I thought using it provided a natural way of creating my segments.

The second step is targeting or picking which segment you are going to go after. If you segment by geography, which area are you going to go after (your own neighborhood, an urban area, suburban area, etc.)? If you segment by price point, what is the price range you are going to go after (first-time buyers, move-up buyers, luxury buyers, etc.)? If you segment by occupation, what occupation will you go after (doctors, attorneys, CPAs, military, etc.)? You must pick a segment where you will be able to position yourself as someone who can add more value to the transaction than anyone else.

I decided to target segments on the Orange Line of the Metro, which runs from New Carrolton, MD, to Vienna, VA, and connects Fairfax County and Arlington to the District of Columbia. Specifically, I focused on the Orange Line stops in the Arlington, VA, area. During the first five stops in Arlington, the Metro runs underground, which gave developers in the 1990s and 2000s a great opportunity for vertical development within walking distance of mass transit. This led to a robust implementation of the live/work/play concept as the first five Metro stops in Arlington (Rosslyn, Courthouse, Clarendon, VA Square, and Ballston) became areas for plenty of apartments, condos, townhomes, offices, retail shops, restaurants, bars, and more. In 2008, the American Planning Association named the area between the Clarendon and Courthouse Metro stops one of the "Great Streets" in America. In this book I will make frequent reference to Clarendon as not only a Metro stop but also the surrounding neighborhood.

Since I had lived in the Clarendon area since 2007, I knew the area well and decided to target that segment of the market. The live/work/play concept helped make Clarendon one of the most desirable areas for homebuyers in North Arlington and all of the Greater DC area. The challenge for real estate agents and homebuyers is finding the inventory. Many homeowners in the area were able to get high rent payments if they decided to rent their homes out instead of selling them when they moved. This was one of the factors that led to low sales turnover in the area. For example, if you are looking for a certain type of two-bedroom condo in one of Clarendon's five condo buildings, you might only get one or two chances a year to buy one. During my years there, I noticed that inventory was low, sales happened quickly, and most of the sales were done by a handful of agents. I knew that my experience living in that area, purchasing multiple condos there, and years observing the market would make that the best place for me to have the highest chance of success as a real estate agent. I think it is critical to target a segment that you really know well.

Finally, the third step after segmenting your market and picking your target is positioning yourself as the person who can add the most value. How can you add more value to that segment of the market than anyone else? Maybe you have lived in that area for years and know it better than anyone else. If you are starting out, maybe you have more time and energy to dedicate to each person personally than an established but overworked agent. If you have a large team and are breaking into a new segment, maybe you have experience in a similar segment that will translate into success in this segment. The way to position yourself to take over a segment of the market is to develop a unique value proposition that others do not have and effectively communicate it to your target market.

The buyers and sellers in my target market tended to be highly educated professionals, so I decided to position myself as a highly educated professional who happened to be in the real estate business. It is not uncommon for real estate agents, even successful ones, to lack education, professionalism, or both. I am not saying that you need advanced degrees to do well in the real estate business. However, I have found it rare for many real estate agents to actively seek out more training and education—whether it be from books, seminars, conferences, and so on. One of the qualities that we look for when hiring agents at the Orange Line Living Team or Keri Shull Team is a strong commitment to lifelong learning. We also look for professionalism, another quality lacking in many agents.

In addition to positioning myself as a well-educated professional, I decided to also position myself as someone with a deep local knowledge and commitment to providing the maximum amount of value. I created a local real estate brand, Orange Line Living, to make it clear that I was focused on real estate along the Orange Line Metro. This provided challenges at first, as I did not have a transaction history to prove my value, so I did have to adjust my strategy accordingly for my first few transactions. Later on, when my transaction history was proven and I could more easily demonstrate my value, I could make adjustments to my overall strategy and expand the segments I targeted.

So in summary, when I used the STP framework for myself, I segmented the market by geographic area. I decided to target my business on Arlington's Orange Line metro area, and to focus even more on the Clarendon Metro stop and the condo building I lived in there. I branded my business as "Orange Line Living" and created a website, livetheorangeline.com, with a blog focused on homes in that area. I started sending postcards to the condo building I lived in and also created a monthly e-mail newsletter that I e-mailed to the residents there. I also hosted a move-up buyer seminar for residents. My blog focused on events in the area and real estate activity. Most of the people living in this area were professionals working in the DC area. I positioned myself as a professional with a military and business background, with a unique, aggressive marketing approach, a passion for results, and a deep knowledge of the local real estate market.

This approach will work for anyone in real estate—from rookies trying to start their careers to seasoned agents and team leaders looking to deepen their existing market penetration or expand into a new area. The rest of the book goes through how I implemented this strategy by examining several of my transactions. Along the way I also highlight quick but important principles. At the end I also provide you with 100 different strategies to try in order to grow your business hyperfast.

Chapter 1:
Finding Sellers with Under-Door Notes

My first year in real estate started off with two buyer clients look-ing to find hard-to-get properties. Both of the buyer clients I was work-ing for in this case were looking for properties in Clarendon that rarely went on the market during a time of year when inventory was season-ally lower than usual. They began their search around Thanksgiving time, which is not when most sellers decide to put their home on the market. Although I lived in the same building as both of these clients, they initially contacted me as a result of direct mail and e-mail.

> **Dan's Tip, Geographic Focus:** Do not be afraid to start off your real estate career by focusing on a geographic area that you live in or one that you know really well. A lot of agents start off in the business by focusing only on their sphere of influence, family, friends, past colleagues, and so on. While that can work, it does have inherent problems. First, they all know you are just starting out and might not be comfortable using an agent without a track record. Second, your efforts will be spread out geographically, which makes it harder to leverage yourself as an expert on a specific neighborhood or area.

My first buyer client, Sam, was looking for a two-bedroom condo in Clarendon. Sam and his wife, Susan, were already living in a one-bedroom condo in Clarendon and wanted to stay in the same area but have more space. Sam and Susan reached out to me after receiving postcards and e-mails that I targeted to the building. In these postcards and e-mails, I positioned myself as an agent who lived in the building, knew the area very well, and had a professional business background. I also offered relevant local news and pricing updates, and I always directed them to my website, at livetheorangeline.com, where I had even more great information about local real estate and the area in general.

They wanted at least two bedrooms and a little bit more space than the typical 1,000-sq.-ft., two-bedroom condo in the area. With a price range in the low 600s, they had to focus on two-bedroom condos in the area because the costs of townhomes were significantly more, even after factoring in the difference in condo fees and homeowners' association (HOA) fees.

> **Dan's Tip, Analyze All Costs and Savings:** When you are analyzing your clients' budgets and what they can afford, make sure you include all factors. The condo and HOA fee can sometimes make a huge difference. For example, if a $600,000 condo has a $600 condo fee, it might actually have a higher cost of ownership than a $700,000 dollar townhome that has a $100 HOA fee.

Before I began showing Sam and Susan homes, I told them about my process and how I work, because I knew that doing so would make our search more effective. This is an important discussion to have with every potential new buyer. Many real estate agents, especially newer ones, are afraid to have this conversation. They just want to show buyers houses. That is an important step, as almost everyone looks at the home they might want to buy before they actually make an offer on it. However, jumping straight to the looking phase without first having the process meeting is a mistake.

After about a month of looking, three different two-bedroom condos came on the market at Clarendon, but they did not work out for various reasons. One was too small. Another one was on the second floor looking directly into a popular bar. The third one was right above the garage for the building and the door frequently going up and down made too much noise for the couple to feel they wanted to make an offer.

With the middle of the winter holiday season coming up, I knew the chances of any more inventory coming on the market would be slim to none. Based on the feedback they gave me about the few places I did show them and our conversations, I had a pretty good idea of the type of place Sam and Susan would like. I decided that rather than waiting for a place to come to me, I would go out and find one.

The building that Sam, Susan, and I lived in, the Phoenix condo, had roughly 180 homes, of which about half were two bedrooms. I knew they preferred a certain height above the street, so that eliminated about three of the 11 floors. I also knew their price range would probably allow them to go up to a unit in size of around 1150 square feet, so I eliminated anything bigger than that. I also eliminated any unit that had been sold within the previous year. After applying these criteria, I was left with about 30 units that would be a good fit for them. I had my targets.

Shortly after doing this, I wrote the following note:

Hello Phoenix Homeowner,
I have a client that is looking for a 2-bedroom condo just like yours. Due to low inventory they have not been able to find anything like this on the active market. If you have any thoughts at all about selling, please contact me at 571-969-7653 or dan@livetheorangeline.com, as I may be able to bring you a great offer and save you the time, costs and hassle of putting your home on the market.
Best,
Dan

With a target of 30, writing these notes by hand can easily be done in an hour or less, which is what I usually did. If I had to target more homes, I would sometimes do a handwritten note and then photocopy it, which I think had the same effect.

I put the handwritten notes in unmarked envelopes and slid them under the doors of the 30 condo homes I targeted. I got an e-mail the next day from someone saying they got my note and were thinking about selling in the next six months. I responded by calling them promptly and scheduling an appointment for the next day.

The next day I met Marissa and her husband, Bob. Marissa was pregnant and had a due date of three months. They had already signed a contract to buy their next home, a new home about an hour away, which would be finished in about four months. They were trying to decide whether to sell their home now, before the baby came, or to wait until after the baby arrived. In either case, they were leaning heavily toward trying to sell it by themselves as a For Sale by Owner (FSBO). Marissa and Bob were very focused on the costs of selling their home (commission), rather than the bottom line.

> **Dan's Tip, Fees vs. Bottom Line:** There are many buyers and sellers who focus on commission rather than how much money they make when selling or how good of a deal they get when buying. If you do not attempt to overcome this objection, you will lose thousands of dollars each year or month in your real estate career. Your prospects will also lose thousands of dollars because you failed to show them the value you could help create. While commission rates are important to sellers, the bottom line they can put in their pocket is more important to them, so you must be able to show them that you can put more money in their pocket and eliminate time and stress for them.

To counter this objection, I presented them with evidence that selling with me would net them more money and save them lots of time. I provided them with examples and statistics in the area of the difference in the prices sellers received in different situations ranging from FSBO to discount brokers to full-service brokers. Since I was starting out in my career, I did not have a portfolio of my own examples to show them. That did not matter. There were plenty of examples of sales in the area showing the results of different sales approaches. I am sure this is true of nearly every area when it comes to real estate, so no matter where you are geographically and no matter what stage of your career you are in, you should have no problem finding examples to show your prospects the financial benefits of using your services. A good way to start finding examples is to look at the sales of other agents in your brokerage and then compare them to the results of FSBO sales and discount brokers. Finding sales in your own brokerage that sold faster or for a higher percentage of list price than FSBO or discount broker sales will give you a record to leverage if you do not yet have your own.

I also created a sense of urgency by telling them I had a client very interested in two-bedroom condos in that area and specifically in that building. If the sellers waited several months, it was very likely that my clients would have found something else to buy. The combination of presenting your value and creating a sense of urgency is very powerful. They said they did not want to sell right away, but the next day they contacted me and said they wanted to meet again to discuss their options for selling now.

Marissa and Bob told me during that meeting that they wanted to take advantage of the low-inventory market and try to sell their home before their baby was due and before more homes came on the market in the Spring. Like most sellers, their biggest concerns were the potential sales price as well as the commission. The price they wanted to list for was higher than the last few sales of homes in the neighborhood. Most sellers believe their home is better than ones that recently sold. It is part of human nature to have this type of bias. We agreed on a price of $625,000, which was about 5% higher than the last sale.

The bigger discussion was about commission. When I met with this couple they thought they could sell their home for top dollar without paying commission to anyone. On rare occasions there are homeowners who can do this. However, most people who try this method of selling their home fail and eventually list their homes with a broker after wasting their time and energy. What Bob and Marissa really overlooked in their initial thinking was the time it would take to sell their home. They would have to do the following activities at a minimum: properly stage and de-clutter their home, take professional-quality photos or hire someone to do the same, perform a thorough market evaluation to develop their list price, develop brochures, post their home on multiple online listing services, develop the most effective descriptions of their home, answer dozens of e-mails and phone calls from buyers and agents, conduct showings at random times, host open houses, familiarize themselves with purchase contracts and laws, negotiate potential offers, coordinate inspections and contingency removals, and scheduling closes. These are only some of the activities involved, and Bob and Marissa both had full-time jobs and were just months away from welcoming their first child and moving to a new home.

As we began our discussion, Marissa and Bob told me that they had been hoping to sell their condo by themselves and pay zero commission. There was no way, they said, that they would ever pay a 6% commission, but after bringing their attention to the bottom line instead of transaction costs—as well as the amount of time and energy they would have to invest to sell it on their own—they began to realize that paying a full-service broker (me) would actually save them time and net them more money. They did not agree to a full 6% commission deal, but they somewhat reluctantly agreed to a commission of 5% with a variable rate of 4% if I were to represent the buyer as well. Many agents might balk at the idea of taking a listing for such a discount.

However, as a new agent just starting out in a low-inventory market, I saw it as a big opportunity on several fronts. One, it gave me a chance to help find my buyer clients a property that no other agent would be able to show them. Two, it gave me an opportunity to get a listing in a high-demand building that had low inventory. Finally, if the sale went through, it would give me an opportunity to market a great sale for the building. It would be the first two-bedroom sale in that building in over six months, the first one of that calendar year, and the highest resale for that type of condo unit since the original building sold out. I knew a successful sale would create an event I could leverage with multiple different marketing messages to get future business. Although getting this listing required me to take a lower commission than I wanted to charge, I was willing to do it because of the different ways I knew this listing could create value for my clients and for me. Although I think this kind of commission reduction is primarily something for beginning agents to do, an established agent or team might also consider it when trying to break into a new market.

After Marissa and Bob committed to working with me on selling their condo, I gave Sam and Susan the good news. They were excited about the possibility of a condo that fit their needs becoming available. They were also excited about the opportunity to see the home before it came on the market. Marissa and Bob got their home ready for the market in a few days. I showed the condo to Sam and Susan the day before listing it. They liked it. It was not 100% perfect for them—few homes ever are—but it met more than 90% of their criteria. The one thing they wanted more than anything was a better view on a higher floor.

The challenge I now faced was their objection to the view. I overcame this objection with a simple analysis of the number of condos that fit their criteria and had a better view. The three or four buildings that had condos that might work for them had roughly 800 total units. A third of those were two-bedroom units in their price range, leaving about 260 units. Of those 260 units, only about half were large enough to fit their size requirements, leaving just 130 units before taking into account the view. Most buildings in that neighborhood have only one side of the four sides that do not directly face another building, which means of the 130 units left, about 35 to 40 of them would not look directly into another building. Since Marissa and Bob's unit was positioned mid-level in the building, only half of the remaining units would be higher, leaving no more than 20 units in the neighborhood they wanted. Since the turnover, or percentage of units that sell in a year, was 10% or less, it seemed very likely that in a year they could only expect at most one or two units like this one, but on a higher floor, to come on the market.

Dan's Tip, Reality Check Analysis: It is important to help your clients understand not only what is actively for sale on the market but also what has historically been on the market and what might come up on the market. I also call this a "reality check analysis." This provides your clients with additional relevant information that enables them to make better decisions in less time. Such an analysis involves doing a search of what has sold in the past year, or more, depending on the turnover of homes. It also involves showing your clients what might come on the market based on the total amount of homes in the area and the average turnover. These factors will help your clients make decisions about pricing and the likelihood of their finding a better home by waiting. If you do not get your clients to the decision point, everyone suffers. Your clients might miss out on the right place and you will not make many sales.

Thus, passing on this condo might lead to a six- to twelve-month wait to find one that was a better fit. After presenting this analysis to them, they decided to write an offer.

Sam and Susan decided to write an offer for $600,000. This number was $25,000 lower than the seller's list price, but there were comparable sales that supported that number. In a good market, most sellers are thrilled to get an offer on the first weekend, but they are usually not thrilled if the offer is 4% below their list price. Although they priced their home aggressively, the lack of inventory gave them justification for doing so. Marissa and Bob decided to counter at $620,000. After thinking about it for another day, Sam and Susan decided to come up to $610,000 and indicated it was their best and final offer.

The next day, Marissa and Bob had their first open house. The turnout was good, but not great. After the first weekend on the market, there was no indication that any other offers were imminent. After much consideration, they decided to counter the buyers' latest offer and come down to $615,000.

It was too little, too late for Sam and Susan. They decided that $610,000 was their best and final and they were actually reaching the point where they were beginning to lose interest even at that level. When I told Marissa and Bob that the buyers were holding firm, they indicated they were done with negotiating and losing interest at getting the deal done and that they did not care if their home was on the market for several months, even though I explained to them they might wait longer and get a lower eventual sales price.

At this point I had a critical decision to make. Both sides were getting fatigued from the negotiations and losing interest in making the sale happen. Marissa and Bob started to show signs of not wanting to negotiate much now or even in the future. I definitely did not want one of my first sales in this building to stay on the market for months— or worse—end as a withdrawal or expired listing. I also knew that if Sam and Susan did not get this condo, it could be several months or more before another one came on the market that met their criteria.

There was only one thing I knew that could create a win–win–win. I offered Sam and Susan a $5,000 credit if they would come up to the $615,000 sales price. This credit would come straight out of my commission. Because of the listing agreement, I was already reducing the commission to 4% for dual agency, so this meant my commission would be just over 3% in this situation. However, I knew that giving up the $5,000 was well worth it—for several reasons:

- It would give me a quick sale at a good number that I could market and use to get more business in the building and surrounding area.
- It would help Sam and Susan not miss out on a place and would prevent their having to spend several more months finding another one.
- It would eliminate the possibility of having a listing go bad.
- It would make both of my clients happy.

Overall, the commission rebate seemed like the best way to create a win for the buyers, for the sellers, and for me. I told Susan and Sam (1) that I believed this was the best condo for them and that the analysis showed it was very likely it could take months or even longer for another one that met their criteria to come on the market, (2) that I wanted them to have such a good experience during the selling process that in the future they would refer me to all their friends and family, and (3) that I was willing to offer them a $5,000 credit because of our being gridlocked in negotiations.

> **Dan's Tip, When to Use Commission to Close a Deal:** There will be several times in your real estate career when you have to decide when it is worth reaching into your own commission in order to get a deal done. It will typically happen more earlier on in your career. It is a judgment call that you have to make based on several items: the likelihood of the deal getting done, the chances of the buyers finding another place if they do not get this one, the chances of the sellers finding another buyer and the potential marketing benefits of getting the deal done. There may be other items you have to evaluate as well when making this decision. It is also important to do it in a way where you give honor to all parties involved, ensure them that they are making a good decision, and ask for referrals and testimonies in return.

Sam and Susan were very happy. So were Marissa and Bob. It was a win for everyone. The contract was signed, and everything went pretty smoothly during the contract period. Then the pre-settlement walk-through inspection took place. There were three issues that came up. First, the HVAC system was not serviced in accordance with what everyone had agreed to during the home inspection. Second, some of the closet shelving had been removed. Finally, the home was nowhere near the level of cleanliness normally expected for home sales in the area.

When I presented the issues to the sellers, they stiffened in their resolve again. While they agreed to bring back the shelving, they did not agree to fix the other two items. Rather than risk a last-minute meltdown or fight, I hired an HVAC company to come service their system. I also spent several hours cleaning their home the night before the sale. As a former Navy submarine officer, I took pride in making sure the job was done right and turning over something that is in tip-top shape. I also bought a gift card to the Container Store so the buyers could get even more shelving if they wanted. Overall, it was a sale that began with a tough negotiating period and ended with a harder-than-normal final walk-through inspection. It was a situation in which everyone could have walked away losing. Instead, because I was persistent and used a little creativity, everyone walked away as a winner.

My second buyer client was another couple. Mike and Julia lived in a condo in Clarendon and were in the same kind of situation as Sam and Susan had been in. They also reached out to me after seeing my e-mails, postcards, and open houses in the building. They wanted more space but wanted to stay close to where they already lived. Their price point was not quite enough for a single-family home in the area, but they could definitely do a townhome. This was a big challenge, though. There were no townhomes in Clarendon listed for sale in the Multiple Listing Service (MLS) at the time, so I showed them all the townhomes available in the next four closest Metro stops. Expanding the search to the next four closest Metro stops revealed four town-homes for sale, but they did not like any of them, primarily because they really wanted to be at the Clarendon Metro stop.

Since location was the problem, I started to look for ways to find townhomes in Clarendon that might work for them. I checked Craigslist, Zillow, Trulia, and other sources. Finally, I found one that an owner posted on Craigslist as a For Sale by Owner (FSBO). I contacted the owner and told her I represented a client looking for a townhome in her neighborhood.

Dan's Tip, Talking to FSBOs: Looking for "For Sale By Owner" homes (FSBOs) has multiple benefits. First, if you have buyer clients interested in the FSBO home you find, you are providing them with a benefit that most real estate agents do not provide. That is, you are giving them access to a home that they might not otherwise see by looking at MLS feeds, Zillow, Trulia, and so on. It shows the client you are being proactive about their search.

Second, there is also the benefit of having engaged a property owner interested in selling their home in a discussion. Maybe that seller will succeed in selling the home, but the odds are definitely against that happening because nearly 90% of all FSBOs eventually use a real estate agent to list and sell their home. Engaging FSBO prospects in conversation and letting them know you have an client interested in their home sends a signal that you are an engaged and proactive real estate agent. Perhaps your clients will buy the home, but if they do not do so you have already entered into a dialogue with the seller. That opens up the possibility of talking about how you can help them successfully sell their home. It also creates an opportunity to find out if that seller knows of any other potential sellers in the neighborhood.

Many real estate agents do not like contacting FSBOs, and such an attitude makes no sense at all. The sellers have made it pretty obvious they are interested in selling their home, so why would you not want to engage them? Too many real estate agents fail to contact FSBOs because they are afraid of rejection, they do not want to "bother" someone, or they are just plain lazy. If these "reasons" are enough to keep you from contacting people who are clearly interested in selling their homes, then you are going to waste opportunities to meet people to whom you can provide value, lose tons of money in potential commissions, and probably not last too long in the real estate profession.

The owner of the FSBO townhome agreed to pay me a buyer agent commission if my client purchased the home. I showed Mike and Julia the home. They loved the location, and the price point was perfect for them, but Julia wanted something that was bigger. I realized I would have to find them an end unit, because tax records for the community showed only end units were bigger in size.

I began to scour every source I could find, and within a few days an end-unit townhome just a few doors down from the first townhome I showed them appeared on Zillow as a Make Me Move (MMM). Zillow MMM homes are listed by owners who are not necessarily interested in selling yet but would take an offer if one came in at the right price. This particular home was listed for $1,125,000. I contacted the owner, Simon, and he agreed to pay me a buyer agent commission if a buyer I represented paid his MMM price.

I set up a showing for Mike and Julia. This home was at least 40% bigger than the townhome I had previously shown them, so I thought they would love it. However, the home did not work for them. Although it was bigger and an end unit, it was located on the inside rows of townhomes and so it did not get a lot of light. I now realized that I needed to find an end unit on the exterior side of the rows so that it would get more light.

This took the challenge to a whole new level. This townhome development had a total of 89 townhomes. Of those, only 11 were end units that would have more light. On average, one of the end units sold every one to two years. I decided to resort to the note strategy again. I wrote a note that said the following:

Dear Clarendon Park Townhome Owner,
I have a client interested in a townhome just like yours. They love the neighborhood and want to have an end unit because they love natural light. As you may know, it has been a while since a home like yours sold. Inventory is low and so are interest rates. Because of these factors, I may be able to get you a great offer with few contingencies and a closing time frame that works perfectly for you. You can also save the time, hassle, and costs of putting your home on the market. Since my clients have a flexible timeline, do not hesitate to contact me even if you think your time frame for selling is further out than

a buyer looking right now might want. If you have any thoughts about selling, please contact me at 571-969-7653 or e-mail dan@livetheorangeline.com. I look forward to hearing from you, Dan"

I put these notes under the doors of the 11 homes that I thought would work for my clients. Within a week I received four phone calls. Two people were interested in selling in the Spring market, and two people were over a year out but were interested in getting a price analysis.

I met with Liam and Janet a few days later. They owned a beautiful end-unit townhome facing the park with views of the Washington Monument, making it an even more rare home. They were definitely going to be selling their home in the next 30 to 60 days but liked the idea of selling it without listing it if possible. I told them that timeline would work with my buyer client. They agreed to a buyer agent commission if one of my clients purchased their home.

Dan's Tip, Selling Off-Market: Many times potential sellers do not want to list their home. Some have timelines that are too far out. Others think they will get more money by not paying a listing commission. These are opportunities you should welcome. If you have met people who do want to sell their home but aren't ready right now, that means that at least you have made contact, one of the most important steps in getting listings. Offer them other services such as pulling comparable sales or bringing buyers to their house if they will agree to a buyer agent commission. The more helpful activity you do the more likely they are to list with you if they decide to list their home.

Within a few days I met with Tom and Theresa. They owned an end-unit townhome a few doors down from Liam and Janet. It was not on the park, but it did have a very nice courtyard entrance and was located nearly as close as you could get to the popular shopping area. They did not want to list their home yet but did agree to pay a buyer agent commission if one of my clients purchased their home.

When I told Mike and Julia that I found not just one but two end-unit townhomes to look at, they were thrilled. I showed them both units, and they loved them both. The unit on the park was the perfect location. The other home had better appliance and other updates though. They decided to go with the less-upgraded home that had the location on the park.

Both owners had stated they wanted to ask for $1.1 million. Mike and Julia decided to write an offer for $1,020,000, nearly $80,000 below the list price. I presented the offer to Liam and Janet, and they decided to write a counteroffer at $1.05 million. Mike and Julia thought about it for a day and decided to make a final offer of $1,035,000. The next day Liam and Janet decided to accept the offer. They got the quick, easy sale they wanted without having to go on the market. Mike and Julia got the perfect townhome they wanted. I got a great sale in one of the most popular neighborhoods in area. It was a win–win–win! Selling two rarely available homes and being involved on both sides of the transaction was a great way to kick off my first year in real estate and right out of the gate put me over $3 million in sales.

Want actionable real estate advice straight from Dan and Keri? Want access to the same videos we use to train our own agents?

At HyperFast Academy, we have an extensive library of video courses on social media marketing, lead generation, crafting winning offers, and so much more!

Visit hyperfastacademy.com to see for yourself!

Chapter 2:
Positioning Through Targeted E-mail Newsletters

I met my next client through a very popular e-newsletter that I created. Using an e-mail newsletter is a great way to get in front of prospects. The key to success with an e-newsletter, like any other type of marketing, is to remember the STP framework. You have to position your newsletter so that it contains interesting, relevant, and compelling information for your target audience. The e-mail newsletter that I sent to the Phoenix condo residents contained information about the area and nearby events, trends in the real estate market, and recent sales and market activity. I also highlighted successful sales I had in the neighborhood and promoted upcoming listings.

My newsletter had great results, often getting readership rates of 50% to 60%, which is two to three times the industry average. I did get the occasional opt-out or e-mail back from someone who was not interested in what I had to say, but the overwhelming response to my e-newsletter was great.

Dan's Tip, Using Lists: Segmented lists are key to having a quick start in developing your real estate business and for long-term success. There are several different ways to segment, including by geography, by people you know, by past clients, and by industry. I still use my Phoenix condo newsletter list. I have also added several other lists over the years, including a past-client list, lists of people who have come to open houses in various neighborhoods, a list of renters in a certain area, and a list of job seekers who are potentially exiting the military. Your lists do not need to be perfect. The key is to develop lists that are segmented so you can target your audience by how you position yourself and your services. The better segmented your list, the easier the rest of the process will be.

In my case, I started by having a list of everyone who owned a condo in a particular building. Being a resident of that building helped in getting my initial lists, but there are several ways that you can get an effective list. It may take a little creativity and doggedness to create your list, but once you have one or more created, you can start to craft messages that will resonate with people, and your sales pipeline will grow.

Steve and Claire first responded to one of my newsletters that had information about the two-bedroom condo that I was about to sell for Bob and Marissa. They were also living in a one-bedroom condo in the Phoenix that Steve bought before marrying Claire. Now that they were combining households, they were ready to get a larger house. They wanted to see the two-bedroom home that my newsletter was promoting as "Coming Soon."

Dan's Tip, Coming Soon: "Coming Soon" is a great marketing tool that will help you get more buyers than any other tool. Buyers want houses. A "Coming Soon" advertisement is compelling because buyers need to contact you to get the most information about the house. In the age of IDX websites, Zillow, Trulia, and other consumer-facing sites, it is very easy for buyers to find out about homes that are actively on the market. While many of these sites do not have accurate and up-to-date information, and none are a replacement for a knowledgeable agent, they do provide consumers with an easy way to get information about homes on the market. However, if a home is "Coming Soon" and is not yet actively listed, the potential buyer's best way to learn more information is to call the agent promoting the home. I learned this early in my career and used "Coming Soon" techniques in e-mail campaigns, direct mail, blog posts, social media, and signs.

I first met Steve and Claire at the two-bedroom condo that Bob and Marissa owned. They liked it, but it was one of the first places they saw, and they were still deciding if they should go with a townhome or a condo. Claire had just sold her old place and moved in with her husband. So now I knew they had each had recent experiences with different real estate agents. I asked them if I could meet them at their home so I could go over a game plan of how to sell their place and find the right next home for them.

You could definitely tell that their home had just gone through a household combination. The one-bedroom condo was bursting at the seams and packed with lots of furniture and household items. Steve had hockey gear everywhere, and we talked a bit together about the NHL. We spent the next several minutes talking about what he and Claire were looking for in their next home. They wanted a home in a location close to stores, restaurants, and parks, but it did not necessarily have to be in the same neighborhood they were in. They wanted enough room so they could have at least two bedrooms plus a home office. They wanted a price point of under $650,000.

After I spent time getting to know their needs, I went through my listing presentation and explained how I could help them achieve their goals. They were in a financial position that would permit them to buy their next home without selling their current one. This was key for them, because then they did not have to worry about all of the excess stuff in their home. Their plan was to buy their next home, move into it, and then stage their old home prior to going on the market. I knew we had at least several weeks before their home would go on the market, so I explained how I would start marketing it now as a "Coming Soon" home, while we looked for their next home. Since they enjoyed seeing homes that were not yet on the market, they were excited about being able to do that with buyers for their home. After we found the right home for them, the game plan would be to get them under contract with a quick close, move their extra stuff out of their current home, and get it staged and on the market as quickly as possible. Until then, I would market their home as a "Coming Soon" listing.

The "Coming Soon" program was one where I began marketing homes before they went into the MLS. There were several ways I did this. I would tell all potential buyers I was working with and talk about the listing at our brokerage's weekly sales meeting so all the other agents in the office knew about it. I would also start marketing the home in direct mail, e-mail newsletters, and social media. This type of extra marketing built up demand before the home was listed in the MLS, and it was something that few agents were doing at the time.

Overall, it went well with Steve and Claire, and they decided to have me represent them in both their purchase of their new home and the sale of their existing home. The following is the three-step process that I would repeat when meeting a potential new client:

1) Establish Rapport: This seems basic enough, but many sales agents fail to do this. Finding things in common with your potential clients will help build emotional connections and make them want to do business with you. It will also make them want to stay in a long-term relationship with you and give you future business and referrals. It is pretty easy to establish rapport with someone. All it takes is finding something about them that you have in common. It can be what occupation they are in, where they are from, where they went to school, what sports they like, what hobbies they have, and so on.

2) Find Out What Needs and Wants They Have: It is hard to help someone if you do not know how you can help them. You have to ask questions and listen. Again, this is fairly simple, but too many people in real estate or in sales fail to do this. They are too concerned with going through their presentation or making their pitch. Many times these types of salespersons are not even listening when the prospects are talking. They are simply waiting to talk. The key to this step is to ask questions about what the person wants and needs, and what motivates them. You must be genuinely interested learning about them.

3) Position Yourself as Uniquely Able to Solve Their Challenges: After you find out what a potential clients needs and wants, you must figure out how you are uniquely able to help them. Here are just a few possibilities:

> • You live in their neighborhood and know it better than anyone else and can help them find a hard-to-get home before it comes on the market.

- Sellers are interested in buyers, so if you are working with more potential buyers in that market than your competition, or if you have lists of buyers, make that known to seller prospects.
- You have more time available than any other agent to help them get their home staged and prepped to go on the market.
- You have a relationship with the lender that has the best loan program available for their financial situation.
- You, or your brokerage or team, have a micro website that has the highest search results for their neighborhood.

Again, these are just a few examples, but the possibilities are endless. You just have to put yourself in your potential customer's position and think about what unique advantage you have that will help the customer. Finally, you must believe you have that advantage and communicate it to the customer. If you do not think you can offer your clients something unique that will help them overcome challenges and get what they want, then you will not be different than any of the thousands of other agents out there and will not earn their business.

I began taking Steve and Claire to several homes in their existing neighborhood. In that area, the townhomes that fit their space criteria started in the range of $650,000 to $750,000. It became very apparent after my second time taking them out that they preferred homes that were a little bit bigger than the ones I was showing them. In order to show them bigger homes, we had to shift gears.

Outside of marketing and presentation, there are really only three things that affect the sale of a home: (1) price, (2) location, and (3) features. Increasing the amount you are willing to pay for a home will give you more flexibility when it comes to choosing the location and features. If you go to a more desired location, your price will go up and vice versa if you go to a less-desired location. The desirability of location can change over time due to development and economic changes. Features include the size of the land and house as well as the age, quality, and amenities. Better features cost more money and vice versa. If buyers are not finding what they are looking for, they will have to make an adjustment to at least one of the three items: price, location, or features. Sometimes it takes a bit of triangulation to narrow down to the right home.

Steve and Claire did not necessarily need the access to the Metro that their current neighborhood in Arlington provided. We started to look at townhomes in the neighboring city of Alexandria, where they found they could get townhomes several hundred square feet bigger with similar features for the same price or even less. The major difference was the location, which was not near a Metro station and not quite as developed as their current neighborhood. As a result of looking in a slightly less-developed area, they were able to look at homes with similar or better features for lower prices.

Steve and Claire found two homes in two different Alexandria neighborhoods. One of the townhomes had just come on the market. The other one had been on the market for a while. They decided to think about the decision overnight. Their decision was made easier because the next day the townhome that had just gone on the market quickly went under contract after receiving multiple offers. They decided to put in an offer on the second townhome.

While it was a seller's market, this particular townhome had been on the market for over a month, so Steve and Claire decided to put in an offer for 5% below list price. The sellers countered the offer, coming down 3% from the list price. During that time another townhome came on the market. It was listed for $550,000 and in the same neighborhood, and it was almost identical to the first townhome Steve and Claire liked. They decided to see that one right away, and they liked it more than any others they had seen so far, including the one they had just made an offer on.

Since the sellers of the first place they made an offer on had countered their offer, Steve and Claire were free to make another offer on a different home without the risk of going under contract on two different places. They did not wait and immediately made an offer on the home that just came on the market.

The last townhome in this community sold after the first weekend on the market and had multiple offers, which bid the price up over the asking price. Steve and Claire were fine with paying the list price, but they did not want to get into a bidding war that would make them escalate in price.

Dan's Tip, How to Avoid the Bidding War by Getting Your Offer in First: Avoiding bidding wars can help reduce your clients' stress and save them time and money—and make them raving fans of yours. While it is not always possible to do this, there are certain things you can do to make it more likely to get them their desired home before it gets bid up in price.

First, get them to see the home as soon as possible. There are several ways to do this. Find out about the home before other agents do, if you can. You can do this by looking at "Coming Soon" sections on Zillow, Trulia, the MLS (if yours has this status), and other websites. Talk to the predominant listing agents in the areas your buyers are looking in and see if they have any upcoming listings. Scour FSBOs. Talk to the doormen in condo buildings. In other words, do everything you can to learn about properties before they come on the market. Knowing ahead of time gives you the best chance of avoiding the bidding war. Even if it is still not possible to avoid the bidding war, the extra time you have will help you and your clients get finances in order, check with lenders, study comps, and do everything possible to put the strongest offer forward.

If your clients like the home and want to get it, call the listing agent and ask if the seller would be able to respond to an offer that day. Sometimes the agent will say yes. If the agent says yes, your follow-up question should be, "Great, what type of offer do you think it would take to get a deal done today? My clients really like the house, and they would like to get it wrapped up today. If we cannot come to a deal quickly, they might want to move on to their second choice." It is important to have this conversation on the phone. It gives you a chance to hear the agent's first reaction. If you do it over e-mail, you will not get the benefit of hearing the agent's first reaction.

Dan's Tip, How to Avoid the Bidding War when the Listing Agent Does not Want to Review Offers Prior to a Deadline: If the agent says the seller will not review offers until some later time, usually a day or two after the first open house, do not give up right away. A great way to follow up that response is to say, "I understand your seller has a deadline to review offers, but my client really likes this home and wanted to know if there would be any offer that would be strong enough to compel the seller to review it now and possibly forgo the deadline."

The agent will most likely not know the answer to this question and will have to call the seller to find out if an early offer would work and at what price. When the agent gets back to you, it will most likely be with one of two possible answers. First, the seller would consider an early offer if certain terms and conditions are met. The second possibility is that the seller wants to stick to an offer deadline no matter what. It is okay if you get the second answer. You did everything you could to try and avoid the bidding war and will now have to turn your focus to doing everything you can to win the bidding war—and without necessarily being the highest-priced offer.

If the seller will accept an early offer, you have given your clients a chance to avoid the bidding war. This is a huge success, but the task is not done until you get a ratified contract. Confirm with the listing agent what terms the seller will accept. This, of course, includes price (you will almost always have to pay at least list price) but may also include having little or no contingencies, such as financing, appraisal, or home inspection. It is important to move fast during this phase because it is likely that there are other buyers who like the home just as much as your clients do.

Steve and Claire decided to write an offer at list price. Since they were pre-approved with a great lender already, they felt comfortable with not having a financing or appraisal contingency. They did include a three-day home inspection. This coincided with the three-day homeowner association review period required by Virginia law, so their home inspection contingency did not actually add any risk to the seller.

While many buyers are afraid to write this type of contract, it is actually a fear rooted in traditional agent thinking. If a buyer has been pre-approved by a great lender, there is usually no reason for financing to fall through. Likewise, if you study the comparable sold homes in the area, are confident of the price, and have a good lender who will use good appraisers, it is very unlikely that the home will not appraise. Many times buyers will benefit more by not having these contingencies in their offer because the seller will respond to the lack of contingencies by being more flexible on price.

As an agent representing a buyer, it is important that early on in the process you talk to the buyer about getting approved with a good lender. It is also important that you take the time to develop relationships with a few different lenders. Make sure the lenders have good response times, quick underwriting times, and the ability to close loans on time. More often than not, the lenders who succeed in this area are not going to come from big national banks, such as Wells Fargo or Bank of America, but are going to be local or regional banks or correspondent lenders.

As a buyer's agent you must talk to your clients early on in the process and get them comfortable with a good lender. This will serve several purposes. First, it will give them an accurate depiction of how much of a loan they can qualify for and what the payments will be. You do not want to waste their time or yours looking at homes above or below their price range. Second, if there are any potential underwriting issues, the lender will be able to catch them early and fix them before the buyer finds a home. Getting a buyer's loan file cleaned up is something that should be done before they start looking for homes rather than after they find the one they want to buy. If you can get your buyers approved up front with a great lender, you will be in a much better place to get them to write an offer without a financing or appraisal contingency. The money they will save by doing this will often be much greater than the perceived risk that the contingencies would be protecting.

The other item to educate your buyers up front about is the home inspection. Many traditional agents believe that having a long home inspection period is necessary. In some cases that may be true, but it is definitely not always the case, and you should present both sides of the equation to your clients so they can make the best choice. If you develop relationships with a few good home inspectors, they will be available to you on short notice, so you should be able to schedule home inspections with 24 to 72 hours' notice. If your clients are looking at a home with a condo or homeowner association, most states have mandatory review periods. These review periods give the buyers a certain amount of time to review the association documents. During this time they can void the contract for any reason. In Virginia, this time period is three days. So if your client wants to get a home inspection, making the home inspection contingency period equal to or less than the time of the association document-review period will make the offer stronger, because the contract would be contingent anyway. While many agents suggest seven to ten days for home inspection periods, that time period weakens the offer because it is extending the total length of time that the sale is contingent. If the offer is weaker in the area of contingencies, that seller is probably going to expect better terms somewhere else in the contract, such as price, or in a competing situation, they will be more likely to pick a different offer. If you do not take the time to develop relationships with high-quality, responsive home inspectors, and if you do not educate your buyers up front about the choices they have with the length of home inspections, then you are limiting their options with this part of the contract. This will prevent them from having an option that might save them thousands of dollars or give them a better chance in a competing-offer situation.

Steve and Claire wrote an offer for the list price. They did not have financing or appraisal contingencies. The townhome was part of a homeowners' association, so they had a three-day review period and decided to make their home inspection period for three days, which avoided extending the length of time the contract would be contingent. The sellers accepted the offer before the first weekend on the market. It was a win–win for everyone. Steve and Claire got the house they wanted, and they did not have to pay over list price. By moving to an area just a little further from their current neighborhood, they were able to spend less money and get a bigger home. The location was still close to plenty of shops, restaurants, and parks, and only a few minutes from Washington, DC. It was a win for the sellers because, although they missed out on a potential bidding war, they got a contract for 100% of the list price with a total contingency period of just three days, which by law was the shortest possible period.

SELLING STEVE AND CLAIRE'S HOME

Steve and Claire closed on their new home within three weeks of ratifying their contract. The home inspection found very few issues with the home, the appraisal came in satisfactory, and the lender got through underwriting very quickly. It was altogether a very uneventful contract-to-close period, which is exactly what you want for yourself and your clients.

During this time we prepared our strategy for going to the market with their current home. The last unit like Steve and Claire's had recently sold for $380,000. We believed it should have gone for more and was not marketed properly. My plan to generate the most buyers looking at their home consisted of getting it staged properly, conducting a pre-market campaign, and then having a great open house and first weekend on the market.

Because Steve and Claire had just combined households, their one-bedroom condo was very cramped and had a lot of furniture. Our plan was to move the majority of their items out as soon as they closed on their new home and to leave behind enough pieces to give buyers an idea of how the space could be used. This is the key to staging a property. If there is too much stuff in a home, it looks cluttered and small. Too many things in a house makes it hard for buyers to imagine how they would fit everything into the space. If the home is completely empty or only has a few items, it makes it hard for buyers to envision how they would use the space. Most buyers have little experience in imagining how they would use a space, so an empty house isn't helpful. As the listing agent, it is important that either you or a staging expert create an atmosphere in the home that will appeal to the majority of buyers and make it easy for them to see themselves living there.

Buying a home is a large—but infrequent—purchase for most people. This makes it hard for buyers to be creative when looking at a home and imagining living there. The purpose of staging is to bridge this gap and make it easy for buyers to see themselves living there. Getting more people to the point where they can imagine themselves living in a home will result in more interest and therefore more offers and a higher sold price.

While we were getting Steve and Claire's home staged, we also started the pre-market campaign. During this phase, I used several different methods to begin letting people know about their home. The home was featured in my e-mail newsletter that went to several hundred people in the neighborhood. I also sent out postcards advertising the home as "Coming soon," and I incorporated the Internet as a part of my strategy, posting the home on my website (www.livetheorange-line.com), Zillow, Trulia, and Craigslist. On Craigslist, I tested multiple types of descriptions and headlines.

Dan's Tip, Using Craigslist with Narrow Ads: On Craigslist it pays to test multiple types of headlines and descriptions of properties. The descriptions can make the ad either wide or narrow. Wider ads will capture more leads, but the leads will have a smaller chance of liking your listing. Narrower ads will capture fewer leads, but the leads will have a higher chance of liking your listing. Examples of descriptive elements that can make your ad wider or narrower are price, size, location, condo building, civic association, and school districts. If you make your headline and description specific, you will get fewer leads. For example, if your description talks about the exact building the listing is in, you will only get buyers who are interested in that building. That's a narrow ad. When a lead contacts you from a narrow ad, there is a greater chance they will be interested in the exact property you are advertising.

Dan's Tip, Using Craigslist with Wide Ads: If the description says the condo is near a certain Metro station, you will get buyers who are interested in any building around that Metro stop. This is an example of what I call a wide ad. It is smart to utilize a mix of both types of advertisements. While the narrow ads are great for generating leads specific to the property being advertised, the wider ads are great because they will generate more leads. These will require more sorting. Some of them will not be interested in the listing but might be interested in another one that you have or another home you know about. You can still help these people even if they do not have any interest in the particular ad they responded to. Some of the people will not be interested in the listing at first but might get there if you take the time to figure out what they want and what they do not want. When someone has an initial objection, you will frequently be able to overcome it or find an alternative solution. For example, if buyers say that they want a three-bedroom condo, ask them how they want to use the third bedroom. Maybe they only need it for an office and so a two-bedroom with den condo could work. Wider ads will cast a bigger net. Some of the people will be interested in the listing and some will not. Sometimes you will find people interested in a listing only after they responded to a wider ad of another listing. The bottom line is that these ads help all of your sellers.

As another part of my strategy for Steve and Claire, I informed the managers of the condo building that Steve and Claire's home would be coming on the market. The managers worked at the desk during the day and evening, so they had a lot of interactions with residents as well as non-residents who walked in off the street. People in these types of positions can do a lot for you, because they meet people during the course of their work. In this case it worked out very well. A few days before the listing went on the market, the night manager introduced me to Dr. Jack, a dentist who had a nearby practice. Dr. Jack was interested in getting an investment property in the area. I showed him the home three days before it went on the market. It was exactly what he was looking for, but he did not agree with the price. Because the last one went for $380,000, he only wanted to make an offer of $385,000. I wrote the offer up for him, but because it was $10,000 below the list price the seller did not want to respond to it until after the open house. Dr. Jack would have to wait, because his offer was not compelling enough to make the seller forgo the open house.

As soon as I put the home on the market, I received several requests from other real estate agents for showings. We received our second offer on the day before the open house. This time it was from an agent, Debbie, representing a first-time homebuyer. The offer came in at $389,000. It was better than Dr. Jack's offer, but still $6,000 below list price. It was not high enough to get a response from Steve and Claire prior to the open house.

On Sunday we had a three-hour open house. In addition to several directional signs with balloons that I had placed near the building and at busy intersections in the adjacent areas, I had marketed the open house via the MLS, online syndicates, my own website (livetheorange-line.com), direct mail, e-mail newsletters, and social media. I made a very simple video on YouTube, which I pushed out in my online ads, e-mail newsletter, and social media. The video was a pretty simple format that I developed. I used professional photos of the condo and had background music along with a simple introduction and closing. It was a very easy format to plug-and-play and reproduce on other listings. The length was no more than two minutes. I think when it comes to virtual video tours, there are two key things to keep in mind. First, keep the video simple. It should not be too long, because people do not have a long attention span online, anyway. It should be easy to make using something like iMovie for the Mac or similar software for the PC. Second, the distribution channels have to be robust. You can make a real "slick" video and put in on YouTube and if no one watches it you might as well have gone golfing instead of making the video. I pushed the video of the home out via Facebook, Twitter, my e-mail newsletter, and my own website. When I posted ads on Craigslist, I also put links to the video there. Before the first weekend was over, I had over 100 views on YouTube. Many agents who post virtual tours on YouTube get less than ten views, so I was able to generate ten times the exposure on this platform alone. Not only is it helpful in selling a particular house but you also have statistical proof of how well your marketing works that you can show to prospective sellers in the future.

During the open house I also had help from a lender who I invited. Having a lender at an open house can help in several ways. First, it gives buyers someone to talk to about loan programs and payments for the home they are standing in. Telling someone the home will cost $2,000 a month and provide a real tax savings of $500 a month makes the home a lot more reachable than telling them it costs $400,000. A net payment of $1,500 a month is a lot more affordable than $400,000. It is also important to make sure that the lenders you invite to open houses have good track records and work for companies that have a great reputation for giving great rates, providing superior service, and closing loans on time.

A second way in which lenders can help out at open houses is with crowd control. Once you get more than a few groups in the house at a time, it is hard to give each of them enough attention to answer their questions and quickly develop rapport. By groups I mean each interested buyer. It is rare for buyers to come alone, as they will often bring spouses, friends, family, and others who might give them advice about their house search. Having a second person there can help tremendously. If you are answering questions to one group, there is another person there to answers questions. People will stay longer in this scenario than if there was one long line of people waiting to talk to you. If you are showing a couple one room and a new group walks in, someone is there to get them to sign in and to get their vital information. Having some backup goes a long way at a busy open house.

Finally, having a lender present also gives you more credibility to buyers. It shows that you prepared more for the open house than most agents. It also shows that you have taken the time to develop relationships with key people in the home buying process.

Overall, the open house was a great success for Steve and Claire. We had over 20 groups come through. One of the last groups to come through was a young couple. Jim and Rachel had moved to the area nearly a year ago and were living in a new apartment. The apartment had given them some rebates on the initial lease, but that was almost up now and it was set to renew at a much higher rate. They saw an open house sign in the area and decided to check it out. We quickly developed a good rapport.

Dan's Tip, Establishing Rapport at Open Houses: I typically established rapport at open houses by asking a couple of basic questions. The first two questions I asked were usually, "How did you find us today?" and "Where do you live now?" These questions are pretty basic and non-threatening, so most people will give you accurate and open answers. The first question helps give you an idea of where they are in buying stage. If they found you because they were out having brunch and saw a sign, they are probably not as far along or serious as people who found you by looking at listings online or at listings their agent sent them. This question also helps give you feedback on what type of marketing is working for driving traffic to your open houses. The second question also gives you a lot of important information. Are they out-of-town visitors moving to the area? Do they rent in the building next door? Do they own a bigger home and are looking to downsize? The question about where they live will tell you a lot about the people and what type of buyers they might be. It will also give you a chance to relate to them in some way. Maybe you live in their neighborhood, used to live in that neighborhood, or have a close friend who lives there. Chances are that no matter what their answer to this question is, it will provide you with some opportunity to relate to them, which is key in establishing trust and rapport.

The condo was very similar to the apartment that Jim and Rachel were currently renting. The building had very similar amenities and was only two blocks away from their current location. Altogether, it was a pretty apples-to-apples comparison. I asked them if they would have any objections to living there if price was not an issue. They said no, so now it was time to move on to price. It was extremely helpful to have a great lender on hand. The lender asked them a few questions and quickly determined they could qualify for a loan.

He then ran them through different loan scenarios, looking at how the payments shifted with each scenario. Jim and Rachel could put as much as 20% down, but they did not necessarily want to liquidate that much money. So the lender calculated scenarios with 20%, 15%, and 10% down payments. He also calculated different scenarios based on 30-year fixed-rate terms and adjustable rate mortgages (ARMs) of five and seven years. ARMs typically have an initial interest rate that is lower than fixed-rate mortgages.

Dan's Tip, Analyzing Different Loan Scenarios with Less than 20% Down: It is important to make sure your prospective buyers know and understand all of the loan options available to them. After the downturn in the real estate market during 2007–2009, ARMs and loans with less than 20% down have gotten a bad reputation in some circles. This is unfortunate, because for many people these types of loans can make a lot of sense and can save homeowners tens of thousands of dollars. A common criticism of the less than 20% down programs is the private mortgage insurance (PMI) that often comes with them. PMI can add several hundreds of dollars a month to the cost of a mortgage, therefore making it a costly option. However, a number of lenders offer ways to put down less than 20% and not have the hefty PMI expenses. One option is to take out a second loan for the difference between the down payment and 20%. The second loan will usually have a slightly higher interest rate, but because the loan is much smaller than the first loan, it usually does not cause a significant increase in monthly cost. Another advantage with going with the second loan strategy is that the buyers have the flexibility to pay off the second loan later, which will reduce their monthly payments and increase their equity. This is a good choice if the buyers think that in the future they will get a bonus, have an opportunity to liquidate investments that they do not want to currently sell, or simply want to save more money now for their new house.

Dan's Tip, Analyzing Different Loan Scenarios with ARMS: ARMs also got a bad rap after 2009 but can make a lot of sense for buyers. The fear with ARMs is that after the initial period, when rates are lower, rates will shoot up and the buyers will not be able to afford the home. However, ARMs can provide an opportunity to save significant amounts of money. Generally speaking, the shorter the initial rate period on an ARM, the lower the initial interest rates are. Although markets will also vary and change, ARMs with initial rate periods of five to ten years can typically save buyers over one full percentage point of interest and sometimes as much as two points. This can save buyers anywhere from 10%–20% of their monthly housing costs.

Yes, it is possible that interest rates can go up after the initial term. However, over half of homeowners sell their home in less than eight years. As many as 25% of homeowners will sell before five years. The reasons vary and can include getting married, having children, having children move out, getting a job promotion, and getting a job relocation. Even when people buy what they think is their forever home they can find themselves moving in a few years. Over a five- to ten-year period, buyers can save tens of thousands of dollars in interest payments by getting an ARM. Many times they pay for the more expensive 30-year fixed-rate loan only to sell the home in a few years.

I'm not saying that everyone should get an ARM. There may be very good reasons for people to get a fixed-rate loan, but often buyers fail to even consider ARMs because of the unfair reputations they got during the last real estate crash. Even worse, they fail to consider them because their lender or real estate agent did not go over that option with them. As their real estate agent, you should present them with the option so they can make the decision from a place of clarity, having known all the facts. Going with an ARM can save them thousands of dollars or help them increase their price range if they cannot find a suitable home in their current price range.

After reviewing similar properties that had sold in the last six months, Jim and Rachel decided to offer $392,000. They knew the recent sale of $380,000 was somewhat of a fluke and that other one-bedroom condos had sold for more. However, they were not comfortable going up to the list price, even though the seller had already received other offers. If someone beat them in price, they would be at peace with it.

On Sunday night after a great open house, I formally presented the three offers to Steve and Claire: the one from Dr. Jack for $385,000, the one from the first-time homebuyer for $389,000, and the one from Jim and Rachel for $392,000. Steve and Claire were not ready to accept any of them. Because they had only been on the market for three days, they were not ready to accept any offer below the list price. Getting three offers right away is a great sign, but it was somewhat unusual to get three offers that quickly and for all of them to be below the list price.

After they thought about it overnight, Steve and Claire asked me to go back to everyone to tell them there were a total of three offers and to make a request for their best and final offer. Jim and Rachel decided to stay put. It was one of the first homes they saw and they had really only been seriously looking for a day. They were fine with passing on this home if someone else beat them.

When I talked to Debbie, the agent representing the first-time homebuyer, I told her that her client would have to come up in price to be in the running and that switching lenders would also help her case. The buyer's initial offer indicated she was going to use USAA for her loan. USAA is a great company for insurance and some banking products. But they fall short of the mark for home loans and have trouble with closing loans in a timely manner. At the time, they were often taking over 60 days to close loans, and most contracts in the Arlington, VA, market at the time were closing around 30 days. I knew this would be a concern for Steve and Claire because their home was empty, and a delay would cost them money. After Debbie consulted with her client, she informed me that her client would increase the offer to $393,000 but would not switch to a different lender.

When I told Dr. Jack that the seller had two other offers and was asking for everyone's final and best offer, his earlier reluctance to pay the list price shifted. His concern now was getting beat out and losing this place. He ran a very good dental practice and was opening up a new office. Spending more time looking for an investment condo would take up the most valuable resource he had, which was his time. His main concerns were getting a good condo that would rent well and locking in a great interest rate, because rates were near all-time lows.

Dr. Jack did not even need to get off the phone with me to take time to think. He decided he would be fine with paying the list price and said he could close in less than 30 days. He did ask if I would find him the first renter and do it for free. I was fine with providing him that extra value (I would normally charge one month's rent to find a tenant for a landlord).

I told Steve and Claire the updated offers from everyone, and they decided to accept Dr. Jack's offer at $395,000. It was $15,000 higher than a nearly identical one sold for two months earlier, so they were happy with the number as well as the financial strength of the buyer and the quick close. Dr. Jack was happy to get his first investment property under contract, and since I agreed to help him find the first tenant, he could now give his attention back to opening up his new office. Before meeting me, he had spent several hours without any success in finding a property.

Overall, it was another win–win–win. The sellers and buyers both achieved their goals. I got another great sale in the Phoenix condo, and because of my having reached out to the managers of the building, I found another buyer client in the process and helped him achieve his goals. My second month of the year continued on the momentum from the first month. The Spring market was not even here yet and I already had seven transaction sides totaling nearly $5 million in sales, a growing sales pipeline, and a market presence that was growing.

Chapter 3:
Leveraging Bidding Wars and Open Houses

After getting Steve and Claire's condo under contract, I immediately focused on finding another place for Jim and Rachel. Because they had just written an offer with me, I knew their interest was at a very high level, and I did not want to lose that momentum. I also wanted to show them that I would do everything I could to find them the right place. It would have been very easy for them to go to another agent at that point, because they had just met me and wrote an offer with me on my own listing and wound up losing. Finally, I knew that since we were getting into March, more homes would be coming on the market and it would not take me long to find something for them.

I met with them the next day and told them I was sorry they lost but that I would do everything I could to find them a great home. Then I shared my next course of action with them, which was to use handwritten notes to contact every one-bedroom condo owner in the building where they had just missed out. They were pleased to hear that and told me they would like to continue working with me but that they did want one concession to the normal buyer broker agreement. There was one property they saw the same weekend, and they wanted me to give them a rebate of half the buyer commission if they bought that home. It was a single-family home that was priced at $599,000. This was a rare find in North Arlington. At the time, there were almost no single-family homes under $600,000, including homes that were teardowns. Builders and investors were often paying over $600,000 to tear down homes and have the land to build new ones they could sell for a profit. The reason for this anomaly was that the seller had started out priced higher than market value. When it originally came on the market, it was priced at over $700,000. Most homes like it were selling between $620,000 and $640,000. Furthermore, the sellers waited too long for price adjustments. Their latest price adjustment brought it down to under $600,000. Had they originally priced it correctly, they would have gotten much more.

I agreed to Jim and Rachel's condition and went to see the home with them. It was a three-level home that had three bedrooms and a full bathroom on the top level as well as a basement that had a separate entrance and another bedroom and bathroom. This home was out of their original price range, but it did have a number of great points that I shared with them. First, unlike a condo, they would have the option down the road of expanding the home if they needed more room. They could lock in the price of the land now, live in a home that met their current needs, and pay money later to expand it if their family grew. Second, if they decided not to renovate it or expand it, the current builder boom might make it easy to sell after two years and make a great profit, and since they would have lived in it for two years their gains would be tax free. Finally, the basement with a separate bedroom, bathroom, and entrance would give them the ability to get extra income by renting out the space. By installing a washer/dryer and small kitchenette, they could get an extra $1,400 a month in rent. This would more than offset the extra payment from the higher list price.

After I reviewed these points with them, as well as recently sold homes in the neighborhood, they decided to offer $560,000 for the home. This was far below the comparable sold properties, but the higher price came with a bigger down payment requirement. This caused Jim and Rachel to have more fear, and they were not in an emotional state to write an offer that the seller would accept. I did help them get comfortable with making the other terms of the offer such that the seller would be more likely to have a positive response. Jim and Rachel decided to go with a short three-day home inspection and to not have an appraisal or financing contingency. (Because their offer was so far below market value, they did not have fear of a low appraisal and they were already pre-approved by a great lender, so they were not worried about financing. Also, since the home was a single-family home and not a condo, there was even less of a likelihood for an issue about financing. Condos traditionally have more issues with financing because of the risks that lenders associate with non–owner-occupied units, commercial units, and units that are delinquent in condo fee payments).

When I presented the offer to the listing agent, she was quite shocked at the number. I pointed out to her that the home had been on the market longer than most homes in the neighborhood were taking to sell. The next day we received news that the seller was countering at $580,000. I thought this was great news. The latest drop in the list price to $599,000 was only a few days old, and it was already a good deal at that price. Even when a property has been on the market for a while, sellers are often reluctant to come down from the list price after a price drop. I saw the counter at $580,000 as a win for Jim and Rachel.

Unfortunately, Jim and Rachel did not see it as a win. The first place they wrote an offer on was under $400,000. This was an increase of 45% in price. The bigger mortgage and higher down payment put them in a state of fear and uncertainty. I reviewed the positive points with them again: the flexibility to add on in the future, the ability to get additional income through renting the basement, and the potential to get a place under market value with tons of upside. I wholeheartedly believed it would be a great deal for them and made this case as persuasively as I could without going to the point of being so pushy that they would have second thoughts about working with me.

Dan's Tip, Overcoming Client Objections: There is a delicate balance that you must develop and maintain when you deal with client objections. Buyers and sellers are often scared. If you let every objection and worry get in the way, they will always have a reason to not act. If that happens, you have not done your job, because they will not have achieved their goals and will continue to miss out. However, if you push too hard, they will want to pull away—even to the point of not working with you. I think the best way to have this balance is to truly have the client's best interest at heart.

Jim and Rachel decided to think about how they would respond to the counter offer. They wanted to give it at least one night. Unfortunately, before the night was over the listing agent sent notice withdrawing the offer. Another buyer had offered the seller full price, and the seller immediately accepted and canceled the counter offer. Just like that the seller sold the place for $20,000 more than Jim and Rachel could have paid if they accepted the counter offer. The seller would now have that $20,000 back in her pocket, and Jim and Rachel were back to square one.

After I had gotten Steve and Claire's one-bedroom under contract, I immediately put out a strong effort to get another one-bedroom listing. I sent postcards to all the one-bedroom homes in the four condo buildings near the Clarendon Metro. The headline on the postcard read, "I just got this condo under contract at a record-setting price, and I have more buyers looking for one just like it!" The text of the card described how I got multiple offers and that some buyers missed out on getting a home. I also put notes under the door of every one-bedroom condo in the Phoenix. The notes read:

Dear Phoenix Condo Owner,

I just got a one-bedroom condo in the building under contract at a record-setting price. Unfortunately, there were several offers, so more than one buyer missed out. I have a client right now looking for a home very similar to yours. If you have any thoughts about selling, please contact me for a no-obligation price analysis. If you have not checked prices in a while, you might be surprised by what my market analysis will reveal. Even if you are not thinking about sell-ing in the immediate future, do not hesitate to contact me, because my clients have flexible timelines. Please contact me at 571-969-7653 or e-mail dan@livetheorangeline.com.

Best,
Dan

A few days later I got an e-mail from Ray. He owned a one-bedroom and den condo and actually lived right across the hall from me. The next day I went to his home to conduct my listing presentation and give him a market analysis. Ray had a government job and was going to take an opportunity with the same department to go work on the West Coast. His timeline was pretty imminent, and he was motivated to sell. His home was bigger than most one-bedroom condos by about 200 square feet and had a den that could be used for a home office or guest room. I also learned he was going to interview two other agents, one of whom was also trying to gain market share in the Phoenix building. Because he had not met with either of them yet, he was determined to not sign a listing agreement until he did so.

Dan's Tip, Going First or Last for Listing Interviews: I have since learned to ask if the prospective sellers are interviewing other agents before scheduling the initial meeting. If they are, it is ideal to try to schedule your meeting after they have met with the other agents. Usually sellers will want to meet with everyone before they decide, so if you go last, you have the best chance of getting them to sign on the spot. Also, even if you offer a ton of more value and have a better track record, it is hard for sellers to realize your worth if they have nothing to compare it to. If you do schedule your appointment last, it is important to get the sellers to commit to not signing anything until they meet with you. A great way to do this is to tell them that you believe your service is so much better than the average agent that you want them to meet with the others first so they can get a baseline. It is also important to tell them that you are going to put a lot of work into preparing a great market analysis. After that, ask them if they can give you their commitment that they will wait to meet with you before making a decision. Most likely they will have no problem saying yes at that time. If they do say yes, it is very unlikely the agents meeting them before you will be able to get them to sign because most people will not want to break their word.

Although Ray was not going to sign at my initial meeting, the meeting did go very well. I shared with him my two recent sales in the building, which had both been at higher prices than any comparable sold condos in the past. I also told him I had clients who had recently missed out on similar places and might be interested in writing an offer. I used this as a way to create some urgency by letting him know that if something else came up on the market that Jim and Rachel could write on that, in which case he would lose a possible buyer for his home. I pressed my two big advantages: my recent two sales at great prices and my current pipeline of buyers, but Ray would not sign.

He still wanted to meet with the other two agents. The next day he was scheduled to meet with two other agents, including the one that had been trying to get market share in the building. Before leaving, I booked an appointment to meet in the day after those two meetings. If you are not the last person the seller is meeting with and you cannot get them to sign, it is important to get their commitment to meet with you again before making their final decision. This will give you a final chance to overcome any objections and help save many listings.

After my meeting with Ray, I contacted Steve and Claire as well as Bob and Marissa. Since both couples were happy with my recent work in selling their homes, they said they would be more than happy to contact Ray and tell them how great a job I did for them. Getting social proof is very powerful. It was one thing for you to tell a potential client about how great you are, even if you can prove it statistically. It is a completely different and better situation when you can get other people to tell potential clients how great you are. Both couples sent Ray an e-mail telling him how hard I worked for them, the creativity of my strategies, and the ultimate proof of the higher prices I was able to get them. They also gave them their phone numbers in case he had any questions. Ray actually did call them both and they further vouched for me.

Two days later I met with Ray again. I learned that he had only met with one of the agents, the one who had been trying to gain market share in the building. However, his work schedule changed and he had to postpone the other meeting by another two days. I was still not going last. We had a really good follow-up meeting. He was happy with the references he spoke with and confident in what I had shown in my previous two sales in the building. He wanted to sign with me, but he did not want to do so until he met with the last agent.

Then I finally found and overcame the last objection. After more questioning, I found out that the other agent had been promising him a buyer and would only charge a buyer commission of 3% if he brought him a buyer. In that scenario, he would potentially save 3% or more than if it went to market. I told him that was great if the guy actually bought it, but if he did not, how did the agent's track record in the building compare to mine? We looked up the agent's stats and not only did he not have a lot of listing experience in general, but he also did not have a history of any listings in the building or nearby buildings. I was coming off two great sales, so if one of my buyers did not buy his home he had a greater chance of getting a better result with me.

He was almost to the point of signing but not quite there. I needed something else that would push him over the edge. I told him that if I also represented the buyer, I would lower my commission rate from 6% to 4.5% if he committed to me right now so I could start working for him immediately. He was there, except he felt bad about canceling the meeting with the other agent. I told him that it was a normal part of the business, and if he already knew he was going to sign with me, it would be more courteous to save the other agent the time of doing more preparation and meeting with him. I even offered to make the call for him if he was not comfortable. Ray decided he would call the other agent later and then signed the listing agreement.

Dan's Tip, Use Social Proof and Statistics to Win Listings: Two productive ways to show your value are to use social proof and statistics when competing for listings. If you have successful sales, get clients to commit to becoming advocates for you. Get their commitment at the time of the sale, when they are most excited about it. That is the time to get testimonials and a commitment to refer clients to you in the future. The more social proof you have, the better. It is also critical to use statistical proof. Know your own statistics and how to use them to put yourself in the best light. It is also critical that you know how to research the statistics of your competition. If you have sold in more neighborhoods in the area and for better prices, share that information with your potential clients. Both of these items can be extremely helpful in winning listings.

Because he kept his home in pristine condition, Ray did not need much time to get his house ready for the market. I helped him only with some light staging items. Given his timeline, we decided to do a one-week pre-marketing period before listing his home. During that time I did my full pre-marketing campaign like I had done on my previous listings: direct mail, e-mail, Internet, and social media. I also alerted the agents in my office and others in the area, including the agents who lost the listing. During the week leading up to it coming on the market, we made it available to show to anyone that wanted to see it.

Jim and Rachel were excited when I told them a new one-bedroom condo was available in the building they liked. They were a little hesitant about the price, though. Ray decided to list his home for $495,000. The bigger living room and extra den made it about 250 square feet bigger than Steve and Claire's condo. The last floor plan like this one sold for $475,000, but it was on the second floor. Ray's condo was four floors higher. Being up higher definitely gave it more natural light and less street noise, although the view did not change substantially because of the adjacent building.

When I showed the condo to Jim and Rachel they liked it, but they were not sure about the price. They did not think it was worth an extra $5,000 per floor and so they wanted to think about it. A few days later another one-bedroom and den condo came on the market for $500,000 in an adjacent building called Station Square.

Jim and Rachel wanted to see the condo at Station Square. In some ways it was very similar to Ray's home in the Phoenix condo. The square footage was roughly the same, except the one in Station Square had a bigger den that had a window and a half-bathroom. Furthermore, this home had condo fees that were about $180 less per month. This did come at a reduction in amenities because it did not have a fitness center or a full-time doorman. The $180-lower condo fee was very attractive to Jim and Rachel because even after factoring in the cost of buying a gym membership, it would save them $150 a month, which was the cost of an extra $35,000 in mortgage payments.

They decided to write an offer on the condo at Station Square. Another one in the building a couple of floors higher had just sold for $515,000, so this home was priced pretty well at $500,000. Jim and Rachel were not quite comfortable with the financials on the home, though. They had concerns about the down payment and the monthly payment. Although the home was cheaper than the single-family home they had just lost out on, it came with a condo fee that added to the monthly expense, and it did not have the ability to bring in extra money through renting extra rooms.

Jim and Rachel wanted to get the condo, but they also wanted to get the closing costs paid by the seller. The condo came on the market Thursday morning, and by that evening I had prepared what would be the winning offer for them. We offered the full list price but asked for the seller to pay 3% of the closing costs for the buyer. Jim and Rachel were going to put down 10%. Normally they would also have to pay another 3% in closings costs for a total cash-to-close of 13%. Getting this reduced to 10% would let them keep almost 25% more cash.

They thought the chances of the seller giving them 3% off on a well-priced condo on the first weekend of the market were very slim. In order to make their offer more compelling, the only contingency they put in the offer was a three-day home inspection, which coincided with the three-day condo document-review period. Although they were using financing, Jim and Rachel did not add an appraisal or financing contingency to the offer. I also included a buyer "love letter" with the offer. In the letter I introduced Jim and Rachel and gave a quick background of where they were from, how they met, and why they loved the home. I also talked about how great I would be to work with and how great their lender was.

> **Dan's Tip, Love Letters:** While they are certainly no guarantee to help, including a love letter from your buyers to the sellers is a great way to add a personal touch to an offer that might have an impact. Sellers can sometimes be sentimental and learning about why the buyers like their house can make them feel better about the sale. It is also important to sell yourself and the lender so they know everyone will be working hard for a smooth closing.

Early on Friday morning we received word that the seller would accept their offer. We later found out from the listing agent that shortly after the seller accepted the offer, they received another one for full price with no seller subsidies. They also had several other requests for showings. The listing agent also told me later that while writing a clean offer (very little contingencies) played a big role, the "love letter" also played a big part. It had turned out that the seller was from the same town as Jim and Rachel and that this had some emotional pull that played a part in getting her to agree to the 3% subsidy instead of countering the offer or waiting for other potential offers. After three attempts, Jim and Rachel got the house they wanted, and they got it for under market value in a highly competitive market. In less than 30 days they closed on their new home and moved out of the apartment. They were now first-time homeowners and would not be subject to increased rental rates. The home turned out to be perfect for them, and my strategies helped them get it for at least $15,000 under market value.

I put Ray's condo on the market the following week. Unfortu-nately, another similar condo came on the market in an adjacent build-ing. This was the second time in a week that another similar home came on the market. We had a great open house as well as a few agent showings over the weekend. One of the agents who showed the home had a client who was very interested in writing an offer but was also torn by the other home that had just gone on the market. They ended up going with that home, making it the second time in just a few days that a buyer interested in Ray's home ended up buying another similar home that had more recently come on the market.

After another week on the market, we received an offer for Ray's home for $10,000 under list price. The price was okay given that Ray's home had been on the market for a few weeks. The offer had contin-gencies for a home inspection, appraisal, and financing approval. The biggest red flag with the offer was that the buyer was using a lender that was an "Internet" mortgage broker. These types of lenders typi-cally compete on rate only and often have service gaps that lead to problems with underwriting the loan, getting good appraisers, and closing on time. Ray decided to counter the offer $5,000 on price and a request for the buyer to also make a loan application with an alternate lender. Our idea here was that if there was a problem with the buyer's Internet lender, we would have a backup in place who we knew would get the job done.

The buyer's agent said his client was willing to come up in price but did not want to make an additional application with an alternate lender. Because Internet lenders compete on rate only, they usually do not have a hard time beating anyone on rate. In the buyer's mind, saving one-eighth of a point on the loan (the equivalent of less than $15 a month) was worth any headaches the lender might cause. Ray agreed to the $490,000 price and to the buyer sticking with his original lender with no backup. He knew there was greater risk that something could go wrong but was willing to accept that risk in order to get a contract price only 1% off his list price.

> **Dan's Tip, Evaluate the Lender:** When you are helping a client evaluate an offer, do not just look at price. You must also evaluate the other terms: contingencies, earnest money deposit, type of financing, and so on. It is especially important to evaluate the lender. Are the lenders local? Do they have a history of closing loans on time? What is their fallout rate? Look for any warning signs. If the seller has been on the market and does not have any other offers, you might have to accept one with a subpar lender, but at a minimum you need to raise this concern during the offer evaluation process.

Ray kept his place spotless and maintained it in near perfect condition, so he was not concerned with the home inspection. Not surprisingly, it came back perfect, and the buyer did not have any repair questions.

The other contingencies, appraisal and financing, proved to be much more problematic. It started with the appraiser. "Internet" lenders tend to use the cheapest appraisal management companies and appraisers. The appraiser they hired in this case worked primarily in an area two hours to the south in Virginia, where the home types and prices were very different.

I anticipated this might be problematic, so I made sure to prepare a thorough information packet to give to the appraiser when I met her to let her into the condo. The packet included recently sold condos in the building as well as ones in similar buildings nearby. I also had a short summary for each comparable unit that pointed out how it compared to each of the recently sold comparable units. For example, there was one on a lower floor that had a view and street-noise exposure that made it less desirable and had only sold for $10,000 less. There was another similar condo that had sold in a building across the street for $20,000 more. It had a better view, where you could see part of the Washington Monument, but was located in a building that had lower-quality finishes in the condos themselves as well as the common areas.

Unfortunately, my efforts did not work. We were shocked when the appraisal came in at $10,000 under the contract price. The appraiser did not give any credit to Ray's unit for being four floors higher when comparing it to the one on the lower level. However, to our complete surprise, when comparing it to the one in the other building that sold for $20,000 higher, she subtracted $40,000 of value for not having as good of a view. In her analysis, she also included smaller one-bedroom condos that did not have the extra den and overall space. It was a completely inaccurate appraisal done by someone who did not know the area very well.

Because the buyer had an appraisal contingency, he gave notice that he wanted the seller to lower the price by $10,000. In this situation Ray faced three choices. He could say no, giving the seller the option to then walk away. He could acquiesce and thereby receive $10,000 less. And finally, he could try to negotiate and meet somewhere in the middle.

Before Ray made that decision, I tried to fight the appraisal. I sent the appraiser my analysis and called her. I explained how we determined the value of Ray's home and asked why she gave a floor adjustment to the unit that sold in the other building but not to the unit in the same exact building. Having not been in either of the units, she could not give a good explanation (yes, appraisers typically do not go into any property except the one they are evaluating). I also explained to her that the one-bedroom condos without dens that were 200 or more square feet smaller should not be considered as comparables. It did not help the case at all. Once an appraiser puts a value on something, it is difficult to get it changed.

It was back to decision time for Ray. He felt strongly that he should not have to drop the price by $10,000 after being on the market for only a few weeks and was not afraid to go back on the market. Unlike VA and FHA appraisals, conventional appraisals do not stick with the property, so if he did have to go back on the market it would not have created potential problems with future buyers. When I told the listing agent that Ray would not drop the price, he told me his buyer would walk away and was not willing to come up one dollar.

My discussion with Ray centered on whether we wanted to try to cut a deal somewhere in the middle or hold the buyer's feet to the fire and see if he would make good on his threat to walk. Ray decided he would not be upset if the buyer walked away, and he had to put his home back on the market. For him, it would be worth it to take on the risks of putting the home back on the market rather than taking a sure loss of $10,000.

I drafted two forms for Ray to sign. One was a release canceling the contract and releasing the buyer's earnest money deposit. The second was an addendum that said that despite the low appraisal, the parties would proceed to settlement at the contract price. I also changed the status in the MLS from "contingent contract" to "active," scheduled an open house, and put in the remarks that the home was coming back on the market pending a signed release. I then sent both forms to the buyer's agent and told them we would need them to sign one of the forms. I could tell by his reaction that I had sparked some real fear.

Within 30 minutes the agent called me back with a proposed solution from him and his client. They wanted to split the $10,000 difference four ways, between both agents and the buyer and seller. Specifically, he and I would each credit $2,500 to the buyer, the seller would come down $2,500 and the buyer would come up $2,500. I decided I would be okay with giving up $2,500. It was a pretty small amount of the total commission, and it would ensure me another quick sale in the building, which would lead to further marketing opportunities.

When I presented the option to Ray, he had mixed feelings. He was uncomfortable with each of us giving up $2,500. He did not want to give up the money, of course, but he also thought I did a great job and did not deserve to give up the money either. After some deliberation, Ray decided to take the deal. We got the necessary paperwork signed and changed the status in the MLS back to "contract" and canceled the open house.

The next hurdle we had to deal with in the transaction was the financing contingency. Even though we were through the appraisal contingency, we still had to get the lender's final approval for the loan to remove the finance contingency. When lenders underwrite a loan, they have to collect several pieces of data on both the individual and the home: income verification, tax returns, bank statements, the appraisal, specific information about the condo or homeowners' association, and more. They have to verify that all of these pieces of information fit into very precise rules and regulations in order to know that Fannie and Freddie will buy the loan after closing. If Fannie and Freddie do not buy the loan, then the bank or investor takes a huge financial hit. This process got more complex and harder to do after a flurry of new rules and regulations in 2009. A few lenders handled these changes well, but many did not.

In this case the buyer's lender was not able to get the loan fully approved within the time frame of the three-week financing contingency. Ray now faced another decision: whether to kick the buyer out of the contract or give him an extension to get his financing fully approved. Since this was the last hurdle to clear and Ray was in a situation where a delay in closing would not be a big deal, Ray decided to press forward with the transaction. He gave the buyer an extension. I called the lender and asked how much more time he would need. The lender told me three days. We decided to go the safer route and gave them a five-day extension to get full financing approval.

The lender delivered the full loan approval in the last hour of the fifth day, and we removed the financing contingency. The contract was now fully non-contingent. The next week went smoothly, and we got to the closing without any more snags. Just as I had done when I sold the other two condos in the building, at each step in the process I sent out cards letting people know I had sold another condo in my target market. When Ray's home hit the market, people in the building and surrounding buildings had already received a Just Listed post-card. I did the same thing when it went under contract and again when it sold. This time, I featured all three of the homes that I had just sold on a postcard. I also highlighted the sales on my e-mail newsletter that I sent out at least monthly. People, both homeowners and other agents in my office, were starting to notice the success I was having. The first quarter of the year was barely over and I was already selling more homes in the area than my competition, many of whom had several decades of experience.

Chapter 4:
Using People to Find Buyers

I met Dr. Joe the same way I met Dr. Jack, through a referral from the assistant manager at the Phoenix condo building. Dr. Joe had been renting for a couple of years and was now considering a purchase. His practice had grown and he was looking to build up some equity and reduce his tax bill by owning rather than renting. Dr. Joe routinely chatted with the assistant manager because she worked at the front desk of the building. She thought he might be interested in Ray's home, so that was one of the first I showed him. He liked it but knew it was not the right home for him.

Like I had done with my previous buyers, I told Dr. Joe that before we saw homes we needed to meet first to go over the process, to discuss how I would represent him, and to detail his search criteria. This is important for every buyer you work with, but even more so with first-time homebuyers.

Dan's Tip, The Buyer Consultation: Having the buyer process meeting up front is important for several reasons. First, it gives you the chance to discover their needs and wants so you can tailor your services to fit those needs and wants. You will be able to find out what they are looking for in their next home, what their budget is, what types of experiences they have had before when buying a home, if they have gotten qualified with a good lender, what their preferred communication style is, and more. In order to provide maximum value to your clients, you need to discover these things first.

Second, having this meeting up front will save you and them time in the long run. Getting them qualified with the right lender will ensure you are looking at homes in the appropriate price range. Finding out what are deal-breakers and what are must-haves (and why) will save you from taking them to see homes they have no chance of buying.

Finally, this meeting will also give you a chance to show them why you are different from other agents and get their loyalty. If you show them everything you will do to help them find and purchase their home—and it provides them with value—they should have no problem signing a buyer agency agreement. If they do hesitate, it will give you the chance to discover and overcome any objections they may have in working with you. This is the real reason most buyer agents do not want to have this meeting up front. They fear rejection. You need to have the confidence to overcome this. It is better to find out their objections in working with you up front, and if they are not going to use a buyer's agent, it is better to find out now than after you e-mailed them listings, made several phone calls, and conducted multiple showings.

After meeting with Dr. Joe, I discovered he wanted a two-bedroom condo. There were five different Metro stops that interested him, and he could be fine with any of them if the condo was the right one. He wanted something that would be spacious and a little unique. He did not like some of the "cookie-cutter" condos.

Although Dr. Joe was a very strong borrower with great income and enough money for a 20% down payment, after speaking with one of the lenders that I recommended to him, he wanted to go with a low down payment FHA option. FHA loans are a great loan option for many first-time homebuyers. For as little as 3.5% down, borrowers can get loans with competitive interest rates, making these a great option for people who do not have the means for a large down payment, or who simply do not want to make a large down payment. Another advantage of FHA loans compared to conventional loans is that they are available to people with lower credit scores. The major drawback is that because the loan has an LTV of over 80%, borrowers have to make a monthly mortgage insurance payment. This payment buys an insurance policy that protects the bank from a default situation, so it is essentially an extra monthly charge that provides no benefits to the borrower.

In Dr. Joe's case, he had the means for a larger down payment but decided that making a larger down payment was not the best way for him to use that money. He knew that investing that money in expanding his medical practice would have a much greater return than the money he could save by making a bigger down payment and getting a different type of loan. By having the buyer meeting with him, I was able to get better parameters on the type of place he wanted to buy and to present to him a loan program that would help him better allocate his resources. He had no problem signing a buyer agreement and was excited to start his home search with me.

Dr. Joe's search involved many more houses than I originally thought it would take. We started off by looking at condos similar to the one he was renting at the time. There was one in particular that I thought he would like. It was an 1100-sq.-ft., two-bedroom home located in the Station Square condo near the Clarendon Metro. It was a corner unit, so it had more space and more light than most of the condos in the area. It also was unique in that it had unfinished ceilings with exposed ductwork. This made the ceilings three feet higher than usual, which made the home feel bigger and provided even more light. He actually saw this home twice before passing on it. Although it was his favorite location, he decided he wanted more space, so I redirected his search to bigger condos.

Searching for bigger condos took us into other Metro stops, but they were still ones that were well within the area of his desired locations. The challenge, though, with bigger condos is that usually you had to look in older buildings to find them. The condos built in the 1970s, 1980s, and 1990s usually had bigger floor plans, because land was much cheaper and developers could afford to make layouts with more space. We looked at several types of larger units. Some had been renovated. Dr. Joe struggled with many of the updated condos because, although they were updated, the renovations were not the kind he would have chosen. This is a common challenge with older homes that have been updated. The updates often are picked according to the taste of the previous owner or owners. Sometimes the updates can actually become outdated.

Some of the condos I showed Dr. Joe had no updates. These offered the benefit of being available at a lower price point. If Dr. Joe bought one like this, the savings would be enough to add his own customized updates and save money. However, even thought these types of homes saved him money overall, it actually costs him more money out of pocket. For example, if he bought a renovated home for $550,000, his down payment would be 3.5% of $550,000, or $19,250. If he bought a home that was not renovated for $520,000, he could bring it up to the level of the renovated home for an additional $20,000. His total costs would be $540,000 so he would have an extra $10,000 of value there. His down payment would be $17,500, but he would have to spend an extra $20,000 on the renovations after closing. This mean his out-of-pocket expense would be $37,500, over $18,000 more than buying the renovated home. Because that kind of money would be so much more valuable if he invested it into his medical practice, buying an older home that had not had a renovation was not an option that interested Dr. Joe.

It took several days of looking at a variety of condos before Dr. Joe figured out what type of condo he really wanted. He did not want to do an extensive renovation, even if it was purely cosmetic. He wanted something newer, but he did not want it to look like the typical condo that goes into an 80-to-400-unit building. Fortunately, there was a new construction project that fit this description.

Rhodes Hill Square was a boutique condo development that was selling at a fast pace. When Dr. Joe first looked at it, the project was nearly half sold. It consisted of three different buildings, each with its own style. One building consisted of single-level condos. Another building consisted of two-level condos. The third building was a mix of both. Dr. Joe liked that the buildings were small and each looked a little different. After looking at several of the models and the available units, he discovered one he really liked. It was a two-level corner unit that had very high ceilings, which allowed tons of natural light in the condo. The layout was an open floor plan, and it even had a third level, its own private rooftop deck with green views. I could tell this would be the one he would finally make an offer on.

The condo home had a list price of $759,900. This was well above the price range Dr. Joe had been considering so far, but it had a number of features that more than made up for the price, in his mind. It was completely new, looked unique, and had nearly twice as much square footage as most of the condos he had looked at previously. Before putting in an offer, he had his parents look at the condo as well. They liked it, but as most people not familiar with the area, they had a little bit of sticker shock. In the suburban area where they lived, that kind of price tag would get you a nice single-family home with a yard and tons more space.

> **Dan's Tip, Advice from Friends and Family:** Family or friends giving input during transactions can be dangerous, and it happens a lot. When buyers seek advice, they are usually looking for affirmation of their decisions. Well-intentioned friends and family can be dangerous, though. Most of these people do not have the experience that a real estate agent has. Even if they have bought and sold several homes, or even if they are agents themselves, they most likely do not have the same up-to-date experience in the area as the agent working in the transaction. It is important to establish boundaries around this issue up front. If not, you run the risk of your client getting "advice" at every step of the transaction, and it is possible that this well-intentioned "advice" could actually be harmful to them.

I made sure I addressed this with Dr. Joe after his parents brought up their concerns about price. I explained in a respectful but firm way that while his parents definitely wanted to help him, they were not in a position to do so and that their advice might actually be costly to him or prevent him from getting what he wanted. The last time they bought a home was several years ago and in a much different area, making it a completely different experience. While their intentions surely were good, they risked hindering his search instead of helping it.

Dr. Joe decided to write an offer on the condo, but he wanted to get $40,000 off the list price. Most of the condos in the area at that time were selling between 97%–98% of list price, so his desire to get over 5% off the list price seemed to be a little bit of a stretch. However, I thought there would be a good way to make it happen. There were two factors that I thought could help.

First, I knew having good rapport with the builder's sales agent would help. Builders and their agents have incentives to give good deals to buyer's agents in the area that might bring them future business. For example, if a buyer walks into a project without an agent, to the builder or the builder's agent this person represents one transaction. However, if a buyer walks into a project with an agent, they now represent potentially multiple transactions. Many people think with new construction they can get a better deal if they do not have an agent because the builder's agent might not have to split the commission. However, that is not actually how the agreements are usually structured. Furthermore, the sales team will usually want to give a better deal to the person with an agent, because they know that if they make that agent look good, the agent will be more likely to come back and bring more clients in the future. I let the sales agent know that I would bring more clients back in the future and would also tell other agents in my office about the project.

The second factor that I knew was at play was finding ways to create value for Dr. Joe that did not involve lowering the sales price. Builders usually like to give incentives that are not reflected in the sales price. Some examples of this are paying for closing costs and giving free upgrades. The builder is better giving up money in those areas than giving it up on the sales price because higher sales prices will help them get better prices on future sales of units in the project.

In order to get the builder a high sales price on paper but still get my client the most value, I structured Dr. Joe's offer with the following terms:

- Sales Price of $749,900 ($10,000 value)
- Seller to Pay Closing Costs Up to 3% ($22,500 value)
- Seller to Include Extra Storage Unit ($7,500 value)
- Seller to Pay One Year of Condo Dues ($5,000 value)

Altogether the offer I created for Dr. Joe had $45,000 of value, but only $10,000 of it came from the list price. We were both very delighted when we found out the seller was going to take the offer. I think Dr. Joe was very surprised, because he had been expecting to receive a counteroffer and thought it would be hard to get the original $40,000 he wanted, let alone $5,000 more. Of course, after Dr. Joe closed on his home the seller was able to successfully use the higher sales price to get more money on other units in the building, so there was value in the deal for the builder as well.

Dr. Joe would close on his home within 30 days. He used the lender I recommend and stuck with the FHA loan program. The builder paid for all the closing costs, and Dr. Joe only had to come up with $22,500 out-of-pocket. His closing occurred without any excitement, which means there were no problems or surprises. The appraisal went fine, and the lender got the loan through underwriting quickly enough to close on time without having a feverish rush at the end. Dr. Joe was very happy with his home and the process in general. In the future, he would later refer multiple customers to me.

In addition to getting referrals from Dr. Joe, in the future I also got referrals from Dr. Jack. In a matter of a couple of months I had already gotten two great clients from my relationship with the assistant manager in the Phoenix condo building. I was also establishing a track record of success in that building that would lead to future business. Through marketing and hard work I would soon spread that track record outward from that building into the surrounding areas.

Chapter 5:
Finding Craigslist Buyers—Competing for Listings

It was now early May, the Spring market had just started to get active, and I was leading my office in sales and commission. I had "capped out" during the third month of the year, which was the fastest anyone had ever done so in company history. This meant that for the rest of the year I would not have to split any commission with the broker or company except for an administrative fee per each transaction. In most real estate offices, sales agents split their commissions with the broker or company until some annual limit is paid to a broker.

I met my next client through Craigslist. Lacey was a young professional working in the DC area and renting a room in a house near Clarendon. About a week before I met her, I was talking to the assistant manager at the Phoenix condo when I noticed a photographer walking into the lobby. I could tell the photographer was there to take photos of a home because he was taking pictures of the common areas, so I asked him which home he was going to photograph. He gave me the unit number, and I was pretty sure it was a one-bedroom home. I discovered it definitely was a one-bedroom condo when I looked up the tax record. Although I wished I had the listing, I became determined to find the buyer for this condo.

I did everything I thought might work to find the buyer. I e-mailed and called people I had met at recent open houses. I called some of my past clients who had bought in the building and asked them if they had any friends who might be looking to buy in the same area. To my surprise, what ended up working was an ad I placed on Craigslist.

The headline was:

"COMING SOON TO THE PHOENIX CONDO! RARELY AVAILABLE LUXURY 1BR!"

In the body of the ad I put:

"Do not miss out on the rare chance to own a 1BR condo in the highly desired Phoenix building just a few blocks from the Clarendon Metro. This home features hardwood floors and stainless steel appliances. Building amenities include swimming pool, exercise room, theater room, concierge and more. Call 571-969-7653 before you miss out."

This ad worked great because it marketed the building, but I left it general enough to not market a specific condo because it was not my listing. I received an e-mail from Lacey less than a day after placing the ad. She requested more information about the condo. I suggested that we set up a time to talk on the phone later that day, and we scheduled a phone call for that evening. When I spoke with Lacey later that night I started by asking her if she had just started her search. I also asked her to tell me more about what she was looking for and what kind of timeline she had. She was in a flexible lease situation, but was ready to get her first place. Lacey had been looking for a few weeks, and another real estate agent had been sending her listings and had done a few showings. I asked her if she had a signed buyer agreement with his brokerage. She had not.

Lacey told me she wanted a one-bedroom condo in Clarendon. She preferred the Phoenix condo building but was open to others. I told her about the previous units I had sold in the Phoenix and explained that I lived there and was always on the lookout for more that were coming on the market. I then told her a little bit about the one I knew would be coming on the market soon. She seemed very excited about that unit. The agent who had been sending her listings never talked about finding homes before they came on the market and kept trying to show her listings in areas she was less excited about.

I also asked Lacey if she had a pre-approval for a loan from a lender yet. She did not. I discussed with her the importance of getting pre-approved by a high-quality lender, especially since the market was competitive for buyers. Chances are good that even if she had seen the right condo come on the market she might not have been in a position to write a competitive offer. The agent who had been sending her listings had failed in doing his job of getting her in the best possible position to get what she wanted.

He also failed to discuss with her the concept of agent representation and had never talked to her about a buyer agency agreement. Because of this, he was not really her agent but was merely someone who was sending her listing information. Lacey felt confident in my ability not only to find her the right place but to also make sure she was prepared to write the offer that would get her the place she wanted. She decided to sign a buyer agency agreement with me, and I sent her the paperwork to sign electronically.

Dan's Tip, Get a Buyer Broker Agreement Signed in Order to Understand Expectations: It is not uncommon for real estate agents to try to work with buyers without a buyer agency agreement in place. The most common reason for this is that they are afraid to ask for a buyer agreement because they think the buyer might say no. They would rather send the buyer listings via e-mail and take them to see homes. Once the buyer finds a home to write an offer on, the agent will put the buyer agency agreement in with the offer paperwork for the buyer to sign. There are several problems with conducting real estate business this way.

First, working without an agreement in place is a real easy way to have a situation in which someone's expectations are not met. It could be the agent's expectations. For example, maybe the buyer will walk into an open house and write an offer with the host agent at the open house. It could also be the buyer's expectations that are not met. For example, maybe when the buyer was assuming the commission would always be paid by the seller, there was actually a shortfall in the commission paid by the seller and now the buyer has to make it up out-of-pocket. These are just a few examples of some of the expectations that might not be met if you do not talk about the buyer agreement and get it signed at the beginning of the process.

Dan's Tip, Get a Buyer Broker Agreement Signed in Order to Save Your Clients Time: Another big reason getting the buyer agreement signed in the beginning is that it gives you a chance to sit down with the buyers and talk to them about the process. Even if they are not first-time homebuyers, this is very important. There is a good chance that if they bought more than a few years ago or in a different area, there will be things different about the process this time. For experienced buyers, it will give you the chance to discover what went right and what went wrong in their past experiences so you can tailor your services to what they need and want. No matter how much or how little experience buyers may have, getting the buyer agreement signed in the beginning will also give you a chance to show buyers the value that you bring to the table and why they should work with you. In the case of Lacey, she realized that I would do more to find out about upcoming listings and take the steps to put her in the best possible position to write a winning offer when the best home for her became available. Having this conversation in the beginning will end up saving you and your clients a lot of time and stress.

Dan's Tip, Get a Buyer Broker Agreement Signed and the Law: Finally and perhaps most importantly, it is critical to get the buyer agreement in place up front because in most states it is the law to do this before showing homes to prospective buyers. The agreement formalizes the relationship. If buyers have reservations about signing, this is actually a good thing, because it will help you discover and address any objections they might have about working with you. If they will absolutely not sign an agreement under any circumstance, then it is better to find out now, before you send them dozens of listings and spend hours showing them homes.

After our call, I put Lacey in touch with a lender who I knew would be able to get her pre-approved quickly and close quickly when the time came for her to put in an offer. The next day she contacted the lender and got pre-approved for a loan. Lacey was now ready to move when she saw the right home come up.

The next day, Thursday, two condos that met her criteria came on the market in Clarendon. One was the home I had told her was coming up in the Phoenix. The other was a one-bedroom condo at a nearby condo, called Clarendon 1021. We saw both of them that night. She decided she wanted to put an offer in on the condo at the Phoenix. Because she had known about it in advance, she had already taken the time to get financially prepared as well as mentally prepared. We had studied comparables and talked about everything involved in the process. The condo was listed at $405,000, but she was prepared to go higher if that was needed.

I called the listing agent and told her I had a very qualified client interested in her listing and asked if the sellers would be able to review an offer in the morning if I got them one. She said no. They were planning on holding the open house on Sunday and waiting until Tuesday to review offers. I asked if there was any type of offer that would compel them to respond now rather than waiting through the weekend. She said it was doubtful, but she would ask them and get back to me. Not soon after she called me back and said the sellers definitely wanted to wait until after the weekend and were sticking with their Tuesday offer deadline. I am not really sure whether I believed her or not that there was not any type of offer they would accept now. Many agents in this type of situation would rather hold the open house for their own lead generation needs, even if it means delaying an offer that might be more than the sellers ever imagined.

I also asked the listing agent if there was any information that might be important to know before writing the offer. She said the sellers would prefer a quick close, because the house they were moving to was already ready. She also said they would like as few contingencies as possible.

So for now we were in a waiting game. It did not make sense to give her an offer now, because it would just give them a chance to shop the offer around over the weekend. On Saturday, another condo came on the market in the area, and I took Lacey to see that one. She liked it, but the original one I showed her was still her favorite. Lacey and I talked about the general terms to offer and decided to wait until after the weekend to reassess before deciding on what to submit.

On Monday I called the listing agent to feel her out. I asked how the open house went and if they were expecting any other offers. Of course, she said the open house was great. She also said that they were expecting two others in addition to ours.

I asked her which agents were writing the offers. She did not tell me the names, but she did tell me which firms they were from. One of the firms was the firm that Debbie worked for. I had seen her the first day, when I showed the condo to Lacey. Debbie was waiting to see it with her client, the same one that wrote an offer on the one-bedroom condo I sold two months earlier. I knew Debbie must have been one of the agents writing the offer. I did not know who the other agent writing the offer would be, but it was valuable knowing that Debbie was the one writing one of the offers.

With all of this information at hand, I was ready to make recommendations to Lacey. My advice was to leave out the financing and appraisal contingencies. She was already pre-approved with a great lender, and I did not think the appraisal would be an issue. She was a little nervous about not doing a home inspection, so I told her to make the contingency period three days. This matched the time she would be allowed to review the condo documents, so it did not add any more risk to the sellers and would not weaken the offer. She had no problem closing under 30 days and neither would the lender, so she decided on a 30-day close.

The last big decision for Lacey to make was what price to offer. With three offers in play Lacey knew she would have to go over list price. The last unit like this one sold for $405,000, but there was a similar unit in a nearby building that was listed at $415,000 and went under contract in less than a week. Although it had not closed yet, it was likely that because it went under contract that quickly it would go for close to or even above the list price.

I had given Lacey the information she needed to make the decision, based on sales comparables. However, this was not the only factor at play. Real estate is not just a financial decision when it comes to buying the house you are going to live in. It is also an emotional decision that fills different emotional needs for different people. My advice to Lacey was to offer the list price and use an escalation clause to go higher if she was willing to do this. The escalation clause tells a seller that the buyer will beat an offer by a certain amount up to a certain limit. The key is deciding what your limit will be.

> **Dan's Tip, Advising Your Clients on Escalation Clauses:** My advice to buyers when deciding how much to offer in a competitive situation is to pick an amount that if they lost by a dollar, they would have no regrets. In other words, the buyers should determine at what price they are comfortable losing out on the house and having an escalation clause that goes just below that number. I show them what comparable homes have sold for, but I do not give them a specific number recommendation. When it comes to competition, you never know how much someone else might offer. If you give a price recommendation to buyers and then they get beat out by a number that they would have been willing to beat, the buyers are going to feel like you misled them. Since buying a home is usually a financial and emotional decision, it is better to let the buyers make the choice of how much to offer or how high to escalate.

Lacey decided she was comfortable going up to $410,000. If someone else beat her, she would be okay with losing out at this level. She wrote the offer for the list price, $405,000, and with an escalation clause where she would increase her price to beat higher offers by $1,000 up to a maximum of $410,000. I thought the offer had a good chance of working out.

When I submitted the offer the night before the deadline, I asked the listing agent how many other offers she received, and she confirmed there were two others in addition to Lacey's offer. I pointed out the strong highlights of Lacey's offer other than price: the lack of any contingencies except for a three-day home inspection, pre-approval from a lender who had already closed two deals in the building that year with my clients, a quick 30-day close, and the overall financial strength of Lacey. Since I knew Debbie was writing one of the other offers with a buyer that insisted on using USAA, I also told the listing agent that no matter what she had put in the offer for a closing time frame, USAA would not be able to close the loan within 60 days. Earlier that day I had called USAA and asked them the current closing time frames for condos, and I was told it was 60 to 70 days. I wanted to make sure the listing agent knew the advantage my client had in terms of using a lender who could deliver on a quick close.

Lacey was nervous waiting overnight, but I told her to remain confident. The next day we heard by noon that the seller picked her offer. It had escalated the full amount, so she would pay $410,000, but she was ecstatic. What really made it great for me was that I found out one of the other offers was actually for $420,000. Because of the way we had structured the offer, the seller picked Lacey's offer over another one that was $10,000 higher. The reason was that the other offer would have needed 60 days to close and it also had an appraisal contingency. The cash value to the seller of closing early was at most $2,500, so even after factoring that in, the other offer provided $7,500 of more value.

However, that offer also contained an element of uncertainty. Since the other offer had an appraisal contingency, the buyer could have the right to renegotiate if the appraisal came in low. The problem with this is that the appraisals usually take two to three weeks to come in and so by that time the seller will usually have less leverage to negotiate terms. By eliminating that risk for the seller, Lacey positioned her offer such that the seller chose it and gave up the possibility of getting $10,000, all because of an appraisal contingency.

The next 30 days went very smoothly for everyone involved in the transaction. The home inspection did not reveal anything significant, and so Lacey removed that contingency. While she did not have an appraisal contingency, the bank still required one, and within a week it was completed and the value supported Lacey's contract price. The closing happened on time, and Lacey was thrilled to move into her new home.

Overall, she was extremely happy. After months of her searching unsuccessfully, I was able to help her get prepared to write a winning offer and get to closing without any problems. By educating her up front about the contract and contingencies I was able to put her in a position to write an offer with non-cash terms strong enough to beat out an offer that was $10,000 higher. Lacey appreciated the assertiveness I used in advocating for her offer and in the future would refer several more clients to me.

While I was busy getting Lacey her home, I was also busy trying to convince Tom and Theresa that I could do the best job of listing their home. Tom and Theresa were one of the townhome owners who contacted me after I put notes under their door. I had shown Mike and Julia their home, but they decided to buy their neighbor's home. At the time, Tom and Theresa were interested in selling their home, but they did not need to put in on the market until later in the Spring market, and they did not want to talk about my listing services until that time.

Although Mike and Julia had bought another home, I did not stop trying to find a buyer for Tom and Theresa. While they were not ready to talk about listing their home yet, they were more than happy for me to bring buyers to their home to do private showings. I knew that the more buyers I could bring by during the next two months, the more likely I would be to get their listing, because they would see my resourcefulness in getting buyers into their home without it even being on the market.

During the next two months I ran Craigslist advertisements geared toward getting buyers interested in townhomes in the Clarendon area. Because I did not have a listing agreement yet, I could not market the home in the same way that I could if I did have a listing agreement. I used ads that had the following types of headlines:

- Find Out About Hard to Find Clarendon Townhomes Before They Go on the Market
- Beat Out the Competition! Find Rarely Available Townhomes Before they Go on the Market
- Private Showings Available for Unique Clarendon Townhomes

When people responded to the ad, I would ask general questions about what type of home they were looking for, when they wanted to move, why they wanted to move, and if they were working with an agent yet. If they were looking for a townhome in the $1 million price range and had the right timing and motivation, I would tell them more details about the home, with the exception of the address. If, after learning more details, they wanted to see the home, I would arrange for a meeting and private showing.

When I met the interested buyers, I would conduct my normal buyer process meeting. Some of the buyers signed buyer agency agreements with me. Some would not sign, but even those who did not would still sign a one-day agreement specific to the house so that they could see it. I was able to generate several private showings for Tom and Theresa, but no one was interested enough to write an offer. The biggest challenge was the price. They wanted to get $1,100,000, even though the townhome a few months earlier had closed for $1,035,000.

When the time came for them to put their home on the market, they decided to interview two other agents, both of whom were long-time agents in the area. One of the agents was someone they knew through a referral of a close friend. The other agent was someone who specialized in that area and used to be their neighbor. This was always their long-term plan, and they did not intend to interview anyone else.

But because I had generated so many off-market showings, they gave me the chance to interview for the job. My presentation went well. Tom and Theresa knew I was a newer agent, so I focused on three things during my presentation. First, I highlighted the success I had recently with sales in the area. All of my condo listings in the area had sold for prices higher than any comparables. I also sold their neighbor's townhome successfully without even going on the market. My track record was shorter than those of my competitors, but I had more recent successes.

I also highlighted my successes before my real estate career and included a résumé with my presentation. This included my time in the Navy as a submarine officer, my MBA from Georgetown University, and my previous career as a defense contractor. This connected well with Tom and Theresa because they both had careers in the military and then later as defense contractors. If you have had several accomplishments before your career in real estate, I believe it is important to highlight that. Having a track record of success in other areas is an indication that you are more likely to have success as an agent and shows you are well rounded. Including a résumé shows that you treat the process with seriousness and respect and that you truly think you are interviewing for the job of selling the client's home.

Finally, I pointed out the success I had in generating buyer leads for their home without even putting the house on the market or giving it full marketing. In the last several weeks, I had generated eight showings for Tom and Theresa. I then reviewed my marketing plan with them to show them how I would generate even more after I listed their home. Like my previous sales, this plan included an extensive direct mailing campaign, blogging and social media, and direct e-mail. Since this was a townhome and not a condo, I had a greater opportunity to use signage as well. This was important because their home was located near high foot traffic areas as well as some busier roads.

Overall, the presentation went well, but they had two big questions at the end and were not convinced to use me yet. Their questions were (1) how much I thought their home would sell for, and (2) how much commission I would charge. In an ideal situation, these are both questions that you would not discuss until they are convinced you are the right person to sell their home. If you discuss comparables with sellers and give them a price estimate, more than likely sellers will think their home should sell for more than the number you tell them. It is basic human nature for many people to think their home is the best on the street. Most people will overestimate their home's advantages and underestimate their home's disadvantages. After hearing your number, often the sellers will continue talking with real estate agents until an agent tells them a number they like. I call this the "buy the listing" strategy. Many real estate agents, knowingly and unknowingly, are guilty of this. After the seller signs with the agent who tells them the highest price, the home will usually sit on the market for weeks and months. The sellers will be shocked that no one thinks their home is as valuable as they do. After some time, the real estate agent will get the courage to ask for a price drop. Usually it is not enough. Eventually one of two things happens: (1) The sellers will either get frustrated and withdraw from the market, or (2) the sellers will get frustrated and drop their price low enough so that it finally sells, almost always at a price lower than if they had priced it correctly from the beginning.

The same scenario often happens with commission when agents are unable to convince sellers of the value they can bring them. As a real estate agent, when you are having your initial meetings with a seller, you must be able to convince them you can do one or more of the following three things:

1. Get them more money for their home.
2. Save them time.
3. Make the process less stressful.

If the seller is not convinced you can do one or more of these three items better than anyone else, then it can become a race to the bottom, and if they do not believe they are getting any value from the agents, they will choose the agent who will do the job for the least amount of money. If you believe you are the best person for the job, and you do not convince the seller of that, then not only will you not get the job but you will be the cause of the seller's not getting the best possible result, because someone who will not deliver as much value as you can will be getting the job.

Dan's Tip, Responding to Questions About Price and Commission: When the sellers ask about the list price and the commission, a great response is to ask, "Do you think that I am the best person for the job of selling your home?" If they say no or they are not sure, it is okay to tell them that the only price recommendation that matters is the one from the agent who they think will do the best job. It is also okay to tell them that if they think you are the best agent for the job, you are sure you will be able to come to an agreement on price and commission and that neither will be an issue.

In the case of Tom and Theresa, this approach did not work. They wanted a price recommendation and a commission answer, and they made it clear that not getting that would make their decision very easy. I was in a situation where I had to have that discussion before they made up their mind on who to use. Having just sold their neighbor's home for $1,035,000, I thought I would be able to get $20,000 to $25,000 more for their home. The sale at $1,035,000 was 2.5% higher than the last one, and I thought I could get a similar jump for their home.

For the commission question, I had a bit of information that helped me develop my strategy. When I was in the process of selling Liam and Janet's home in the private sale to Mike and Julia, I found out from them that the same agent who Tom and Theresa were speaking to offered to sell their home for 5.25% if it went on the market. I had a hunch that it was a rate he consistently offered to people in the neighborhood. I decided prior to the meeting that if I could not get Tom and Theresa to commit to me before talking about commission, I would quote them 5.0%. When I did so, they both seem intrigued and told me they would get back to me within a day. I left the meeting thinking I was going to land another million-dollar townhome listing.

The next day I was working in my office with a colleague when all of a sudden Tom walked into the office. He began talking even with my colleague right there and told me that it was a close choice but that they had chosen the other agent. I was surprised, because I thought they were going to pick me, but I was even more surprised to hear this right in front of other agents in the office. However, I did not let the shock show. I immediately asked Tom if he could clarify more. When he started to talk I told him it would be better if we could go in a private room. He agreed and I grabbed my laptop and went into a private conference room.

Tom told me that he and Theresa felt more comfortable with an agent who had more experience and that the agent had agreed to match the 5.0% commission I had offered. I did not let this stop me. Instead, I spent the next hour making my case to Tom and going into my marketing strategy in even more detail than I did in my listing presentation. I showed him more details about my website. In the span of only a few months I had leveraged the standard website my broker offered with a really great blog that was connected with Facebook, YouTube, and other social media. I compared this with the other agent's site. In terms of content and how the property was displayed, there was no match. My site displayed the home's features better and was easier to navigate. Because of the time I had put into blogging and using social media to talk about the area, my site also appeared higher in search results. Since over 90% of homebuyers find their home initially online I stressed the importance of driving more people to the home on the Internet and presenting it in its best possible light to the people who see it.

I also showed Tom more details about my direct mail postcards and flyers. Again, I did a direct comparison to what the other agent was doing and pointed out that there was no match. I spent more money on this and used a better marketing company, and the results showed.

After about 45 minutes of talking about marketing, I could see that Tom was starting to question his decision. I knew I had an opening, and so I made the following case to Tom. I asked him who he thought would work harder to get him a great result: an agent who was somewhat new to the neighborhood or an agent who had done several transactions there before. I made the argument that an agent without a track record in the neighborhood had more to lose and would therefore work harder. The reasoning was that if I messed up one of my first deals in the neighborhood, I might never get another crack at it. Agents with an extensive record can better afford to mess up a deal or two because they have a track record to fall back on.

This seemed to really resonate with Tom. He told me that in hindsight he should have gone with me but thought it was too late. I asked him if he had already signed a listing agreement with the other agent. He said they had agreed verbally, but they were going to actually sign the paperwork later that day. In that moment, I knew I had one last chance and I had to do something dramatic. I decided to cut my commission to 4%, beating the other agent by a full percentage point. Of course I would have liked to have gotten the listing at a higher commission, and I thought my value justified it. However, like my initial listing in the Phoenix condo, I knew getting a listing in Clarendon Park would have a lot of future value for me. Not only would I not lose the listing but I would get the chance to meet owners in the community who would be selling in the future as well as meeting buyers who might buy this home or other homes with me.

I told Tom that I believed I could do a better job for him but that I failed at convincing him and his wife of that. I also told him that doing a great job at selling his home would mean a lot to me, not only because I wanted to provide them with great service but also because I knew it would give me the chance to help their neighbors in the future.

It is important to tell sellers why you are willing to cut commission or give a rebate when you are going to offer that. If you do not understand why you are doing what you propose to do, you can look desperate to them, which is a turnoff. They may also think you are less vested in the sale of their home, so it is important for you to tell them about the value you will get from selling their home at a reduced commission.

I then told Tom I was willing to drop my commission to 4% if they would sign immediately so I could get to work for them. I could tell Tom no longer had any doubt. But he did ask if I had permission from the broker to do that, because he was worried that the broker would not get his split of the commission. I explained to Tom that I had "capped" out my commission split in the first three months of the year, which was something no one had ever done before. Since I was "capped" out, I had complete discretion with what to do here. The fact that I "capped" out so quickly impressed Tom even more. He called Theresa to explain what had happened and confirm the decision. She said she would be home in 30 minutes and asked if we could meet her there. Less than an hour after Tom came into the agent work area and told me in front of other agents that they had not picked me, I walked out of the private conference room through that space en route to his home to sign the listing agreement. My perseverance since meeting this couple paid off, and now I was about to get my second million-dollar listing in my first few months as a full-time agent, and this all started with handwritten notes that I placed under fewer than 12 doors.

After my meeting with Tom, I prepared a listing agreement and then went and met with him and his wife at their home. While we were there, we laid out a specific plan for marketing and timing. They kept their home in immaculate condition, and so there was not a whole lot of preparation needed other than a little bit of decluttering and moving some extra items and pieces of furniture into storage. We decided to go on the market in ten days. During the next ten days, I would aggressively market their home. This would include "Coming Soon" signs on their home and "Coming Soon" directionals throughout the neighborhood. I would also do my usual direct mail, online, social media, and e-mail campaigns. We decided that anyone who expressed interest in seeing the home before it went on the market would be directed to a two-hour showing window two days before their home went live on the MLS. The reason for this was to get multiple motivated buyers in the home at the same time so they would see each other and feel a sense of urgency and competition.

Tom and Theresa were very comfortable with my marketing plan, and we had one more important item to discuss. That was the price. They thought their home should go for $1.1 million. I thought $1,050,000–$1,060,000 was more realistic. Out of curiosity, I asked them what the other agent had recommended. They told me his recommendation was $1,040,000. I told them we could beat his recommendation, but not by as much as they were thinking. They did not want to budge from the $1.1 million. I told them I was fine with that, but I wanted them to commit to a $30,000 price drop if we did not get offers within the first 30 days of being on the market. Tom and Theresa agreed to that, we finished up the listing agreement, and I got to work for them.

During the next ten days I aggressively marketed their home. As I had done before, I sent an e-mail featuring the home to my database, which now consisted of hundreds of people either already living in the area or who had expressed an interest in living in the area. In addition to sending the "Coming Soon" e-mail to potential buyers, I sent it to the top 100 agents who had represented buyers in the area in the last 12 months. It is very easy to create this kind of list using the MLS. I also did my usual Craigslist ads, blogging, social media, and post-cards.

The marketing efforts worked, and I received five requests from people who wanted to see the home before it went on the market. Two of the requests came from real estate agents who got the e-mail blast. Two requests came from people who called after seeing the sign. Another request came from someone who saw the home on Craigslist.

Tom and Theresa were very excited about having five potential buyers. Two days before their home went on the market, I showed the home to all five of the buyers. Their home looked great, and I felt certain that we would get a great offer before we listed it. However, it did not work out that way. None of the buyers liked it enough to pay 6% more for it than the one that I sold a few months ago.

Two days later, the home went on the market, and we had more agent showings. Two days after that we had our first open house. The Spring weather was perfectly cool and sunny, and the flowers and trees were all at the height of their bloom. In addition to marketing the home during the "Coming Soon" period, I marketed the open house on all of my marketing channels. On the morning of the open house, I put out 20 directional signs with balloons. Many agents do not use balloons, but I have found they help draw more attention and let people know the signs are meant for an event that is going on right now. As a result, I think they draw more traffic. That day I had over 40 groups of people come through the open house. It was a very good mix of neighbors and buyers interested in the neighborhood and in the home.

Between the pre-market showings, agent showings, and the open house, I had over 60 groups come through the home during the first four days on the market. The sellers were very pleased. Again I felt certain we would get an offer within a day or two after the open house. I knew the home was priced high, but I thought with the amount of traffic I generated there would be at least one offer.

During the two days after the open house, I followed up with the agents who had shown the home and none of them had clients that were going to write an offer. I sent e-mails and called everyone from the open house, and the results were the same. I was a little surprised, but the sellers were completely shocked, because they were expecting an offer.

During the next few weeks we continued to get similar results. Every week we would get several agent showings, and on the weekends I would host an open house and get anywhere from 20 to 40 groups coming through the home. I also started using ads on Facebook to promote the open houses, and I placed ads in a luxury home magazine. Despite these additional efforts, after 30 days on the market we still did not have any offers.

It was at this point that I was feeling very happy that I previously had the price drop conversation with the sellers. Because they had already committed to a price drop after we reached 30 days on the market, it was much easier to have that conversation now. I reminded Tom and Theresa of my original price recommendation. I had previously recommended a list price of no higher than $1,075,000 and told them I thought the best range would be in the $1,050,000–$1,060,000 range.

> **Dan's Tip, Price Drops:** No one wants to drop a price, but if you have to do it, make sure you take full advantage of this opportunity. You should also treat the price drop as a new marketing opportunity, similar to a new listing, which is why I recommend doing them toward the end of the week on days new listings typically come out. Make sure before you do the drop that you alert any interested buyers and agents, and use the drop as leverage to get them to make an offer. If they are on the fence, the threat of new buyers coming to see the home at a lower price might compel them to write an offer. Make sure you fully market the price drop and drive traffic just like you would if it were a new listing.

Because I had already had this conversation and gotten their commitment to a price drop, I did not have trouble getting Tom and Theresa to drop the price to $1,075,000. I planned on dropping the price on a Thursday so we would have enough time to market the price drop for the open houses over the weekend. Two days before the price drop, I called all of the agents who had showed the home recently to let them know that the price drop was coming. The reason for this is to give them time to go to their clients and see if that might make any impact on an offer decision. You are basically using the pending price drop to put pressure on them to make an offer before the price drop generates more traffic and showings.

On Thursday, I made the price drop for Tom and Theresa. I did more online and social media marketing. I also sent e-mails to agents and my prospect database alerting them to the price drop. The marketing worked, and we had an uptick in showings and a better open house. There was one couple at the open house who seemed very interested. They were already working with an agent, so after the open house I followed up with him and let him know that his clients really liked the home.

The next day the couple from the open house came back to see the home with their real estate agent. They stayed for over two hours, a very good sign. Later that night we received an offer. The good part was that the offer was all cash, with only a home inspection contingency and an appraisal contingency. The bad part was the offer was for $1,035,000, $40,000 below the new list price. I made sure to follow up with the recent showings and interested open house visitors, but there were no takers.

When I discussed the offer with Tom and Theresa they were happy to have received the offer, but they did not like the price. The buyer had offered exactly what the last home like theirs had sold for a few months ago. They believed that their home was nicer and that demand was stronger because it was later in the Spring. The cash part of the offer was nice because it would mean there would not be problems with getting a loan. However, much of the attractiveness of an all-cash offer was diminished because they still wanted an appraisal contingency.

An appraisal contingency on an all-cash offer is different than one on an offer with financing. When financing is involved, the lender or an appraisal management company, hires the appraiser. In an all-cash contract, there is no lender, so the appraiser is hired directly by the buyer. Many people argue that there is actually more risk to the seller in this situation because it is in the buyer's best interest to pick an appraiser who will reduce the price.

Because Tom and Theresa had concerns about both the appraisal and the price, I told them my advice was to counter both terms. They decided to write a counteroffer at $1,055,000 and with no appraisal contingency. The buyers decided to accept the price, but wanted to keep the appraisal contingency.

Tom and Theresa were a little unsure about what to do. They were happy with the overall price. It was in the maximum range I told them initially and was over $15,000 higher than what the agent who used to live in the neighborhood told them it would sell for. However, the appraisal contingency still made them nervous. They asked me what we could do to mitigate the chance of a low appraisal. I suggested two things. The first was that we could insist the appraisal was done by someone from a local Arlington office. I thought it would be a lot less likely to get a bad appraisal if the person doing it did a lot of business locally, because that person's reputation would be on the line.

Second, I explained to Tom and Theresa how I would put together a packet for the appraiser showing how we justified our price. The packet would include recent sales and explanations of those sales that showed how our home compared to other homes. This is something that appraisers have to do anyway, but giving them information like this does three things. First, it shows them that you put some effort into coming up with a logical basis for your price. Second, it might make their job easier. In a busy market, appraisers are sometimes doing as many as ten or more appraisals in a day. This means they not only have to visit that many homes but they also have to look up comparable homes for each home they visit. If you hand them a packet with comparables that are favorable for your list price, they might be inclined to use those rather than do the work of looking for more, which could uncover comparables that are less favorable. Third, if an appraiser has to visit many homes in a day, the human element makes it more likely they will favor the agent who actually showed up, because now they can connect a face to that property.

After having this discussion with Tom and Theresa, they decided to take the offer at $1,055,000 and accept the appraisal contingency.

Now I was only two contingencies, the home inspection and the appraisal, away from getting my second sale of the year at Clarendon Park, both of which would be the highest sales there in several years.

The buyers completed the home inspection a few days later. Tom and Theresa had done a great job over the years with the upkeep of their home, so very few issues came up. After agreeing to a few minor repairs, the home inspection contingency was removed and we were now left dealing with only the appraisal.

A few days later I met the appraiser at the home. The buyers had selected a very reputable Arlington appraiser who had a lot of experience in the area. Tom, Theresa, and I were very happy with the selection. When I met the appraiser there, I had a thoroughly prepared packet that contained other comparables. I included the one in the same neighborhood that I had sold for $20,000 less a few months ago. Because the appraiser cannot access the inside of other comparables, I listed the things in that home that were not as nice as this home. Tom and Theresa's home had an upgraded kitchen with stainless steel appliances and granite counters, an extra fireplace on the main level, and hardwood floors throughout instead of only on the main level. I also included comparables from townhomes in adjacent Metro stops that supported our price point.

The meeting seemed to go well, but it usually takes a day or two before the appraisal report is delivered. The next day we received great news. The appraiser had agreed with the value, the contingencies were now cleared, and the contract was hard. Two weeks later, Tom and Theresa closed on the sale of their home, and they got a price that was $10,000 to $15,000 higher than their old neighborhood real estate agent had told them. They were ecstatic and said they would definitely refer others in the neighborhood to me.

It was really a proud moment for me as well. It all began by placing a random note under their door when I was trying to find a home for a client. At first they intended to sell their home on their own or use a real estate agent they already knew. By working hard to bring them buyers before the home was on the market, I got my foot in the door. After initially making a great listing presentation, I did not get the job, but I refused to take no for an answer. I made a smart cut on my commission to get the job because I knew it would provide value in others ways. The sellers wanted to try for a higher price, so it took longer to sell, but through hard work I got it done.

The choice of cutting commission rates can be tough at times. I do believe that when it comes down to that, you have failed to convince the seller of your value. However, there are times when it does make sense to do this. In this case, here are the advantages I gained by reducing my rate in order to get the job. First, I gained an opportunity to get consecutive sales in a very desired neighborhood with more than $1 million price points. I thought it was worth it to sacrifice now in order to become one of the top two agents in a highly desired neighborhood. Second, I knew the listing would give me a chance to meet a lot of potential buyers and sellers as well as neighbors. I held several open houses there and got to meet over 200 people in a month's time. Several hundred more also saw my postcards, blogs, and signs. Finally, I knew if I did a good job it would give me another advocate for future referrals. Tom and Theresa said they would be more than happy to recommend me to other people they knew and that if any prospective seller was ever on the fence, they would be glad to call them to recommend me.

May was a great month for me. I added another sale at the Phoenix condo, and I got a listing in the Clarendon Park townhomes. As I was approaching the halfway mark on the year, I was now the highest-selling agent in the Clarendon Metro area and on my way to becoming the highest-selling agent in the ZIP code. As my sales increased I continued to expand my marketing in the area. I was determined to continue expanding my market share.

Chapter 6:
Open Houses: Finding Buyers and Selling Listings

My next four sales all came at the Phoenix condo. The multifaceted marketing strategy I developed was working. One of the sales I got was the result of putting a note under someone's door. Another was the result of a Google AdWords campaign. The other two were the result of an open house. All were in my target focus area.

When I sold Marissa and Bob's condo five months earlier, I still had other clients looking for two-bedroom condos. As soon as I got Marissa and Bob's place under contract, I put notes under two doors of other two-bedroom condos that were in similar price points. The notes had my message about how I just got a similar condo under contract for a great price and had other buyers looking for condos like theirs. No one responded, though. A month later, when Marissa and Bob's condo closed, I put similar notes out again. This time I got an e-mail from Alana. She and her sister were moving out of the condo they shared and would need to sell it within the next few months.

I met with them both a few days later. I learned that Alana's father had bought the condo a few years ago, and Alana and her sister lived there while going to school. Alana said they wanted to move in June after the end of the school year, because they would be graduating and then moving on to graduate school in a different area.

In an ideal situation, my meeting would have been with Alana's father because he was the owner and decision maker. It is much more challenging to give a listing presentation when a key decision maker is not present. You can give a great presentation and convince people that you can provide value above and beyond what anyone else can do, but if they do not bring that message back to the decision maker in the same convincing manner, your message will be lost. The other major challenge with not having the key decision maker present is you will not get a chance to learn what their objections are and have an opportunity to overcome them.

My meeting with Alana and her sister went well. I explained my marketing strategy and went over my past sales in the building. I wanted to make sure they had proof of my results to take back to their father in order to establish my credibility. I also took the time to learn their school and work schedules so I could explain how to make showings as least intrusive as possible. In addition to scheduling showings, I thought maintaining the condo in showing condition would be harder then normal. They both did not seem to pick up very much after themselves and had done very little maintenance in the three years they lived there. They also had a pet cat. All of these things added up to a condo that was far from presentable to potential buyers. I showed them several pictures and pieces of marketing material from other condos I had sold. I thought that would be the best way to gently tell them what a place in showing condition should look like. Overall, my presentation went well. I established myself as someone with expertise in the building, went over a great marketing strategy, and developed rapport with the sisters. The one thing I did not do at this meeting was talk price or commission. I was saving that for when Alana and her father were closer to the decision point.

However, I could not get them to sign, because they did not have the authority to do so. I asked them how their father would make his decision. They did not know exactly, and told me they would discuss it with him and when he was ready to sign they would give me instructions on how to send it to him for his electronic signature. I asked if a phone call would be possible, but they told me he did not speak English, so it would not be possible.

I left the meeting feeling good about how things went, given the circumstances, but I knew that without a signed listing agreement and without knowing how the key decision maker felt about me it was far from a done deal. I knew the best thing to do in cases like this was to follow up early and often, and so that is what I did. When I got home that night, I immediately wrote a thank-you note to Alana and her sister. It was nothing fancy. I simply thanked them for taking the time to meet with me and told them that if I got the privilege of selling their home, I would work hard for them and their father. The next morning I delivered the note under their door.

> **Dan's Tip, Following Up After Listing Meetings:** After you meet with a potential seller, you need to follow up early and often. People are busy, and you need to show them you care. If you are not willing to follow up with them after you meet with them for the first time, how can they expect you to follow up with them after they sign the listing agreement or to follow up with agents and buyers when their house is on the market? Your follow-up needs to address any unanswered questions from your initial meeting and anything else that will show them your value. Use it as a chance to further impress them with your professionalism.

I continued to follow up with them for the next two weeks. I sent e-mails asking if they needed any more information and asking how the discussions went with their father. I also called and left voicemails. Finally, about two weeks later Alana contacted me and wanted to meet again.

When we met the next day, it was only Alana. Her younger sister was not there. Alana had talked with her father extensively. She had also met with a real estate agent who was a family friend and also spoke the same language as her father. These are both hard things to compete with if you do not take the appropriate steps to uncover the financial risk to the prospective seller. I asked Alana who the agent was, and she told me. Then I began to look up his results on the MLS, both on the listing side and the buy side. I was not surprised to find out that he had not done any business in the immediate neighborhood, and I shared this information with Alana and her sister. Even when I expanded the search parameters to several miles out from the area, he had not done much business. I asked Alana what kind of price he had quoted them. The list price he recommended was actually tens of thousands of dollars less than a recent one had just sold for. I also found out that he offered to sell their home for 4% commission.

Alana told me that her father wanted to go with the agent he was familiar with and take a 4% commission. I told Alana I was concerned that the agent's lack of previous business in the area would cost them thousands of dollars. I also told her his recommended list price was very low. This, of course, led to her asking me how much I thought the home should be listed for. The last thing I wanted was to give her my recommended list price and then have her father list their home with their friend at the price I thought the home could get. I told Alana I would be more than happy to give her my recommendation on price, but before I did that I wanted to know if she was committed to recommending me to her father.

Alana told me she would have no problem recommending me to her father. She respected my record in the building, liked the fact that I lived in the same building, and had felt comfortable with me. I showed her a recent comparable that had sold for $570,000. This comparable was a floor plan exactly the same as hers, and it had sold a few weeks ago. The unit was located one floor below hers and had a similar view. I told her I could get the same price if they would commit to doing the following things.

They needed to get their home professionally painted. When they moved in, they painted the walls with bright pinks and blues. While they certainly enjoyed these colors, they were not colors that most buyers would appreciate. They also painted the walls themselves and did not do a great job. There were streaks in the walls, places where the paint did not cover, and several places where the colored paint got on the trim. I had a contractor who had helped several people in the building and told her I would be glad to recommend him.

They also needed to hire someone to do a thorough deep cleaning. They had not done a good job of cleaning and upkeep, and it showed. If they wanted to get the same price as the recently sold unit, they would have to make it look as pristine as that home did.

In addition to painting and deep cleaning, there were a few other items they needed to do. First, I recommend they replace both the bedroom carpets. The carpets had excessive damage caused by their cat and by their own attempts at painting. They also needed to remove a lot of their clothing and personal belongings. Alana and her sister simply had too much stuff and it created the impression that their condo was small and bursting at the seams. Finally, I recommended they find a way to keep their cat somewhere else during showings and open houses.

I explained to Alana that if they committed to doing those things and had me marketing and selling their home, they would stand to make tens of thousands of dollars more than if they sold their home through their father's friend. Alana decided to call her father on the spot. They talked at length in another language. At one point I could tell he asked her a question that she did not know how to answer. Of course, it was the commission question, because I still had not gone over that with Alana. At this point I knew I was very close to getting a commitment. I told Alana my rate was 6% and that I knew it was 2% higher than the other agent they spoke with last week. However, I told her that if they listened to my advice on how to get their home ready for the market and if they listed with me, my results would more than make up for the difference.

Alana explained that to her father. When she was done speaking, there seemed to be a pause for a while. After a minute, her father spoke. Alana asked me if I would do it for 5%. I told Alana that I would not go that low, but if she and her sister would commit to doing the things that I recommended, I would list their home for 5.5%. She spoke to her father again. A minute later she told me he decided to list the home with me, but he wanted to list it at $580,000, ten thousand dollars higher than I recommended. I cautioned them against that price but they did not listen. Nonetheless, I was glad that I got my fourth listing of the year in the building.

After Alana got off the phone with her father, I went through the listing paperwork with her to make sure we got the details right. When we finished, I sent it to her father for his electronic signature. I then went over specific details with her on how to get her home ready for market. They wanted to get on the market as soon as possible. Alana had a cleaning service, so she would be able to schedule a deep cleaning the following weekend. In between then and now we would have the condo painted. I had a contractor in the building that had done work for other clients before, so when I called he was able to rearrange his schedule to start the painting in two days, enough time to have it completed for the deep clean. Alana said she and her sister could put some of their items in storage and de-clutter over the weekend. I also gave her the name of a great carpet company so she could get the bedroom carpets replaced that week. We would have the photographer scheduled for early the following week, so we would have enough time to get their home on the market in just over a week. Like my listings before, I would immediately start a complete marketing campaign (online, e-mail, direct mail, social media).

A few days later, I received a phone call from Richard. Richard and his wife, Leslie, owned a two-bedroom condo in the Phoenix. He had seen one of my ads on Google and received my e-mail newsletter as well. Richard had received a job transfer, and he and his wife were planning on moving out of the area. They wanted to meet with me to talk about selling their home. I asked Richard if they were talking to any other agents and was happy to find out that they were not.

When I met with Richard and Leslie the next day, I was very happy to find that they kept their home in great shape. They did not need to move out for another four months. Most condos at the time were taking 30 days or less to sell, so they did not need to put their home on the market for a couple of months. I went over the listing presentation and strategy with them. They were very receptive and seemed to be familiar with most of my marketing already. They remembered seeing me on Google ads, e-mails, postcards, and directional signs in the neighborhood. When I asked them at the end if they were committed to using me, they said yes and we signed a listing agreement for a 6% commission. I just got my fifth listing of the year in the building, which represented over two-thirds of the market share.

Because Richard and Leslie did not need to move for about four months, we decided to put their home on the market in about a month. They had a little bit of work to do in the meantime to get their home ready. One bedroom needed painting. They also had a little bit of decluttering and organizing to do, but overall their home was close to market-ready. In the meantime, I would have an extended period of time before listing the home to market it and build up interest. Their home was a little bit smaller than the one that recently sold for $570,000 and did not have quite as nice of a view, so we decided on a price point of $560,000.

Two days before the photos were scheduled for Alana's condo, I went to check on it to see how the preparation for the market had been going. I thought it would be a quick inspection and maybe involve giving her a few quick last-minute tips. Unfortunately, that was not the case. The painting had been completed, but not much else had been done. I asked Alana when she scheduled the carpet replacement, because the worn carpets were still there. She told me that after talking with her father they decided to "save" money by not getting the carpets replaced. I asked her if she had gotten a deep clean over the weekend. She told me her cleaning service had come, but it was apparent that they had not done anything close to a deep clean. The closets were still messy. So were kitchen appliances. There was dirt and dust build-up on every return air vent for the HVAC system. I told Alana the condo still needed a lot of work and that if she did not get it in better condition, they would probably get lower offers and be on the market for longer. Alana made it clear that she and her sister would not be able to do anything else to get the condo ready because they had tests that week in school.

I could tell that Alana and her sister were not going to do what it took to get their place ready for the market. With less than two days to go before pictures, I did not have time to take chances. I scheduled a professional carpet cleaner to come the next day. Before the carpet cleaner arrived I spent nearly two hours in their condo vacuuming, cleaning, and straightening up. While the place did not look nearly as good as some of my other listings, by the end of the day it was ready enough for pictures.

When I first thought about getting into real estate, cleaning other people's houses was not something I thought about. I thought about negotiating and about helping people figure out financing and marketing. Vacuuming someone else's HVAC vents, organizing people's closets, and organizing someone else's personal items were not things I imagined I would be doing. However, I have always taken pride in my work, and when I listed a home I considered it to be a reflection of me. I was not going to let the condo be in bad shape for the photos that would be used in all of the marketing. That would look bad for the sellers and for me. Yes, cleaning someone else's home was not what I had in mind when I got into real estate, but I knew this was not the time to think I was above this work. I had a condo to sell in the building in which I was beginning to build dominating marketing share, and I took a "get it done" attitude toward making the home look good its visual presentation to the public. There are other options, of course, than doing it yourself. Later on in my career, when I had more listings, I would contract out cleaning services when needed and make the sellers pay for it. When you are starting out, though, you might find yourself in situations where you have to get your hands dirty.

The next day, when the photographer came, the place looked great for the photos. I launched my usual pre-market campaign and received a lot of interest. During the first open house, I had over 20 groups come to the condo. Unfortunately, between the time of the photos and the first open house, the condition of the condo degraded somewhat. When I got there to set up for the open house, there were clothes and personal items scattered around and items left out in the kitchen. Alana and her sister did not find another place to keep their cat either. I did the best I could to make it presentable on such short notice, but most of the people coming through the open house commented that it did not look like the current owners took good care of the condo.

It was clear from people's reactions that no one who saw the home at the first open house was going to buy it. Although the differences between the condition of this home and that others I sold were very small, they were enough to make people not have the fear of loss in them that someone else would buy the home. What would it take to get the home in the same condition as the others? About $1,000 in carpet replacements, $250 for a deep cleaning service, $150 for an HVAC servicing, and a nominal amount to a pet sitter to take their cat. Even though these items were less than $1,500, they would make all the difference in the world to prospective buyers.

During the open house I did meet one buyer, Emily, who loved the building but was not sure about what type of home she wanted. She had just started her first job in Washington, DC, and was looking to buy her first home near a Metro stop in Arlington. She did not really know what type of home she could afford or how much she could get approved for when she applied for a loan. I explained to her that I could definitely help her figure out how to translate the sales price of homes into what the monthly payment would be, and I could put her in touch with some of the area's best loan officers. I also let her know that I had sold several condos in the building and was a resident in the building myself, so I knew the building and area very well. Overall, I established a very good rapport with Emily; however, since she was not really in a state of urgency, I was unable to set a follow-up appointment with her.

After the open house, I gave Alana and her sister a report of how it went. We drove a lot of traffic to the open house, but most of the comments indicated the appearance was going to be a serious obstacle for potential buyers to overcome. When a home looks clean, put together, and not crammed with things, buyers can more easily imagine themselves living in it. When a home looks messy, disorganized, and unkempt, the imaginations of potential buyers work against their buying it. They start wondering what else is wrong with the home and where would they put all of their stuff because the seller does not seem to have enough room. I told Alana that despite the high turnout at the open house, the appearance of the condo turned off any interested buyers. I got the same feedback from agents that had conducted private showings. I did my best to stress to Alana the importance of keeping a great appearance. My pleas fell on deaf ears, though, as Alana told me they were too busy with school to do anything about the appearance of the home.

The next week Richard and Leslie finished the work on getting their home ready for the market. They got the painting done that they needed and had professional cleaners do a complete deep clean. Their home was well organized, and extra belongings had been stored somewhere else. When I went to look at their home the day before their pictures were scheduled, I was pleased to find I would not have to return with cleaning equipment. Their home was ready to go! The pictures turned out great, and we were ten days away from listing their home. Meanwhile, I started my usual pre-market strategy in marketing their home.

A few days later I held the second open house for Alana and her sister. Again, I was able to market the home through social media, online channels, and directional signs. The turnout was not as good as the first week, but it was still very good. We had 15 groups come through this time. One couple I met, Steven and Lauren, were very interested in buying a two-bedroom condo in the area. They already lived nearby but were looking for an investment home. Steven and Lauren had recently sold an investment condo in another area and were looking to use a 1031 exchange to buy another condo.

I could go on at length in the nature of 1031 exchanges, but that is beyond the scope of this book. Basically, a 1031 exchange is a way to sell one investment home and use the proceeds to purchase another investment home. They provide a big tax advantage in that you get to defer the capital gains tax you would normally pay when selling a home. However, there are very strict rules and timelines you must follow during the process. The money has to be held by a third party after the first sale and before the subsequent purchase. The next property you buy has to be identified within 45 days of the sale of the original property, and it has to be purchased within 180 days of the original sale. As a real estate agent, it is important to know this because if a prospective buyer tells you they have sold a property and are trying to conduct a 1031 exchange, they are usually running up against the clock. They have a sense of urgency.

Steven and Lauren were in that situation, and I knew they would have to find a property soon. With the limited inventory in the area, they did not have much to choose from, either. They really liked the building and all of the amenities and thought it was in a great location for attracting renters. Their main problem, though, was the appearance of the condo. Alana and her sister did nothing to improve the appearance of their home since the last open house. If anything, it had actually gotten worse. I asked them several times if they thought they could see the home working for them if we got a deep clean, replaced the rugs, and got a thorough home inspection. Despite my efforts, they said no, and I realized there was no way they were going to buy the home we were standing in.

However, I did think it was very likely they would be interested in a two-bedroom condo on the same floor if it was in great condition. I knew just the place. I told Steven and Lauren there was another condo that might be perfect for them, and then I began to describe Richard and Leslie's home. Steven and Lauren thought it sounded great and asked when they could see it. I told them it would not be on the market for another week, but if they wanted to I could arrange for a private showing. They asked if they could see it later that day after the open house was finished. I shot a quick text message to Richard to see if that would work. When he replied yes, I set the appointment up with Richard and Leslie.

About an hour later, after my open house was finished, I met Steven and Lauren to show them the other condo. Richard and Leslie did a great job in tidying up, even on short notice, and the place look great, a stark difference from Alana's home. Steven and Lauren both really liked the home and thought it was in great shape. They began asking me how much it would rent for and I went over rental comparables with them. I told them it would probably get $3,000 or maybe a little more per month. They seemed to like those numbers.

The next day Steven and Lauren called me early in the morning. They wanted to put an offer in on Richard and Leslie's condo. Based on the square footage difference of other recent sales, Steven and Lauren thought the condo was worth $550,000, about ten thousand less than the anticipated list price. The sale of their other home was going to create enough cash proceeds that they could offer cash and not have an appraisal or financing contingency. In order to help create extra value for everyone, I suggested Steven and Lauren close quickly and then let Richard and Leslie rent the condo back until they needed to move.

This created value in several different ways. First, it made the move easier for Richard and Leslie. They would be able to sell their home quickly and not have to deal with the hassle of keeping it on the market. They could then rent the house back for another two months; right up until the day they needed to move out. Second, it would line up the rental cycle better for Steven and Lauren. Since sellers would be renting the home back, Steven and Lauren would have more time to find their long-term tenant. It would also put them on the summer-to-summer rental cycle, which is one of the better times to look for tenants. Finally, the timeline would work well with the 1031 exchange timelines that Steven and Lauren had to work with for the purchase.

When I took the offer to Richard and Leslie, they were excited to get an offer. They were a little disappointed in a price that was $10,000 under the list price. However, they did recognize the value of having the quick closing and the rent-back period. It would certainly make their life a lot easier during the move. They also liked the certainty of not having a financing or appraisal contingency. All of those items had enough value to them that they decided they would rather take the offer than wait to go on the market and risk the buyers going elsewhere.

This was certainly a win for everyone involved. Steven and Lauren got a great investment home and would be able to meet their 1031 exchange timelines. Because of the rent-back period, I was able to find them a great renter who moved in right when Richard and Leslie moved out. That renter was actually referred to me by my client Lacey, who just moved into the building and was thrilled by the idea of having people she knew move in there as well. The renter ended up staying for several years, making it a great investment for Steven and Lauren. Richard and Leslie were thrilled with the deal because it saved them the hassle from going on the market, they did not have to worry about appraisal or financing contingencies, and they got to live in their home right up until the moment their job transfer took place.

For me it was also a win. I got to help out two clients and found a way to create extra value for both of them. I also was able to sell a listing at a great price before it ever went on the market, which would give me more marketing opportunities and a bigger track record of success. Even though I had been a full-time agent for less than half a year, I was already selling more in my area than agents who had been doing it for 20 or more years. My listings were selling faster than the market average—and for higher prices. I had helped buyers win in bidding wars and buy homes before they came on the market. I started marketing my results to more and more people through more and more channels, which was starting to bring me more and more clients.

I felt that if I could do a better job than the average agent, I had a moral obligation to try and help as many people as possible.

Before my next open house for Alana and her sister, I shared with them the results I had for Richard and Leslie. I did this for two reasons. First, I wanted to show them the difference it made to buyers when they walked into a home with a clean and organized appearance compared to a disorganized and messy home. I figured this proof source might create enough leverage to get them to get their place showing well. Second, I also wanted to give them a proof source of a recent success I had. In a low-inventory market, sellers can get nervous and second-guess their listing choice if their home is on the market for even just a few weeks. I knew it was likely that they were not communicating with their father about the condition of their condo, so I wanted to make sure they had a recent proof source of my success.

I also e-mailed Emily and told her I had just sold a condo before it went on the market and that condos in the area she was looking at were selling fast. In my e-mail I stressed the importance of working with an agent who could not only alert her to condos as soon as they came on the market but also tell her about condos that were "Coming Soon." In other words, I wanted to give her a heads-up on homes that might work for her before they came on the MLS. This would help her potentially avoid bidding wars or at the least give her a head start in preparing a competitive offer for bidding wars. I was able to deliver on this promise because of the listings I was getting in her top building choice and because other listing agents were now telling me about their upcoming listings because they knew about the business I was now doing.

Emily responded and said she was ready to see houses the next weekend. She had not seen many condos outside of the Phoenix building, and so we decided to check out nearby alternatives where there might be a little more inventory. On Saturday I took Emily and her parents around to see about six different condos. They were in buildings ranging from five years old to some over 30 years old. All of them were within a mile of the Phoenix building. The older buildings did not work for Emily. Even though she could get more square footage for the same amount of money, the layouts were not as open and she did not want something that was dated or needed renovations. We also looked at newer buildings at Metro stops only one or two stops away from Clarendon. While she liked some of these buildings, she really did not like the location as much as Clarendon. All signs pointed toward Emily wanting to buy in a newer building in Clarendon.

The next weekend I was able to convince Alana and her father to drop their list price from $580,000 to $550,000, based on my other sale in the building. I also stressed the importance to Alana and her sister to get their home in the best possible shape because the price drop would probably attract a new group of buyers and give them a chance to make a good first impression.

On Saturday I showed the one-bedroom condo to Emily and her family. She liked everything about it and wanted to put in an offer. It was priced at $415,000, a price that I thought would draw multiple offers. I called the listing agent and asked her if her client would review an offer today if I got her one. She said they were going to wait until Monday to review all offers. I asked if there was an offer that would compel the seller to act now. After conferring with her clients, the agent got back to me and told me we would have to wait because the seller did not want to review any offers ahead of time.

On Sunday I showed up an hour early for the open house for Alana's place, and unfortunately the home was not clean or organized. Once again, there were clothes everywhere, food left out, cat litter boxes not changed, and other messes. I spent the next 45 minutes trying to get the place into a reasonable state for the open house. While it was better by the time of the open house, it was far from being in tip-top shape. The open house was very busy, with several buyers as well as a few who were accompanied by their agents. One agent contacted me shortly after the open house, asked me when the seller wanted to close, and told me his client was considering an offer.

On Monday morning I reviewed the final offer strategy with Emily. I told her the property was likely to escalate over the list price and she should think about how much she would be willing to go over the list price and if she would be willing to write an offer with very few contingencies in order to get a better price. Emily decided to make the offer with no appraisal or financing contingencies. The comparable recent sales supported the list price, so she was not concerned about the appraisal and she was already approved from a very reputable lender. She decided to make her escalation clause go up to $420,000, or $5,000 above the list price. Her home inspection contingency had a short period of only three days. It was a very clean offer that would make the sellers feel very good if they decided to take it.

Later that night, we heard back on Emily's offer. The sellers decided to take it. The price escalated to the $420,000 mark, but the sellers chose her offer over one that was $5,000 higher. The key factor in this decision was the lack of the appraisal contingency; the other offer had the contingency. Emily was thrilled, and I was happy for her. I was also pleased to have been able to help her beat out another buyer even though her offer price was lower. It was the second time in two months I had done that.

Dan's Tip, Reducing Seller Risk to Save Buyers Money: Many times the difference between a winning offer and a losing offer, or getting the seller to accept a lower price, is a matter of reducing the amount of risk to the seller. Contingencies add risk to the seller. You can reduce risk to the seller by having fewer contingencies in a contract. If your buyer is not comfortable without having contingencies, you can reduce risk to the seller by shortening the time period for the contingencies. Other ways that reduce risk to the seller include putting down a bigger earnest money deposit or having a bigger down payment. There are other ways that may apply to your situation. The key to remember is that if you can reduce the risks to sellers and create more appealing non-financial terms, they will be more willing to negotiate on the financial terms.

I also received an offer that night for Alana's home. It was at $530,000, which was $20,000 below the list price. I told the agent that I was surprised to see such a low offer and that, while the condo did not show well, it was certainly in great shape and priced below recent comparable sales. When I presented the offer to Alana, she was disappointed. Again, I told her the main difference between her home and other recent sales was the presentation. She relayed this to her father on the phone, and they told me they would accept $540,000, but nothing less. I suggested a counteroffer strategy of presenting a bottom number of $543,000.

When I presented the counteroffer to the buyer's agent, I told him I had to do a lot of work to get the sellers down to that number and that I did not think they would come down any lower. I also reminded him that it was already priced below the last one that sold. The next day his client agreed to the price at $543,000. My clients were happy to have the extra $3,000 but disappointed in the time it took to sell and the overall price. A few weeks later we closed.

I walked away knowing I had done the best I could for them. I had an aggressive marketing strategy, conducted several great open houses, and attempted several times to get them to maintain their home in presentation shape, even cleaning it myself before the photo shoot and each open house. They made the mistake of not following my pricing recommendation in the beginning and not keeping the condo in presentable shape. It was a great lesson on the effects of price and presentation on getting a listing to sell. Although it was not a sale that would be great to market in the building, it still was great for me for several reasons. First, the open houses helped me find a buyer for another listing I had in the building that I was able to sell with zero days on the market. Second, it helped me find a buyer who bought a different condo in the building. Third, it helped me find several buyers who would buy with me in the future. Finally, while the sales price was not something I would want to market in the building, it did add to the total number of sales I had in the building as well as give me several chances to meet more neighbors during open houses.

Adding four more sales in June in the Phoenix condo solidified my market share position even more. I had now had nearly three-quarters of the market share in that building and was on track to have over $20 million in sales for the year.

Chapter 7:
Buying Your Own Listings

My next sale was also in the Phoenix building. One day in early July when I was walking in the lobby, Paul, a resident I often saw in the gym, came up to me and asked me if I could tell him a likely selling price for his condo, because he had just gone under contract to buy a new single-family home. He said he knew me from the gym, had seen my signs at open houses, and received my e-newsletter. I told him we should make an appointment, and he wanted to meet that night. My schedule was free, so I agreed.

When I did the research on Paul's condo, I was both excited and challenged. He owned a one-of-a-kind three-bedroom condo with a huge outdoor terrace. The condo had over 2200 square feet of indoor living space plus an 800-sq.-ft. terrace. The indoor space alone was more than twice as big as the average condo in the area, and a terrace that big was truly unique. Being on the tenth floor, it had breathtaking views. So that was the exciting part.

The challenging part would be determining what price to recommend. Paul bought the condo four years earlier from the developer for $1 million. There were no other condos in that price range in Clarendon. There were a few condos in other Metro stops nearby that sold for over a million, but most of those were in super-luxurious buildings with amenities such as valet parking and private elevators. In the Clarendon area, there had not been another condo sold for over $800,000 in the previous three years.

I decided to use a technique called parallel analysis. In this type of analysis, I would look at the price smaller condos were selling for at the time Paul purchased his condo and compare that to the price they were selling for now. When I did that I discovered that in the four-year period, smaller condos in the same building had appreciated roughly 15%. Applying that percentage of increase to Paul's condo would mean it should sell for $1,150,000.

> **Dan's Tip, Pricing Unique Homes:** When you come across a unique home, it can be challenging to find appropriate comparable sales. One technique that can help is called parallel analysis. To do such an analysis, you must find another nearby home or group of homes and figure out the price they sold at around the time of the last sale of the subject property. Next, you find out how much those homes have gone up in value since the last sale date. Finally, you apply that percentage increase to the subject home to get the recommended price.
>
> Another technique is to expand your geographic area and look at alternatives that are similar in size and features but in a different area. For this to work, though, the area must be similar to the area of your subject home. In other words, it must be an area that would attract the same kind of buyer. There are other methods that will work in pricing a unique home, but these are two of the best.

Parallel analysis is great, but it is far from perfect. For one thing, it assumed that Paul had paid market price for his condo when he bought it from the developer. At the time he purchased the condo, it was still a very rare type of purchase. It is possible the developer could have underpriced it. In this case, Paul's condo would be worth more now than my analysis showed. It is also possible that Paul could have overpaid, in which case his condo would now be worth less than my analysis indicated. The condition of Paul's condo would also have a big impact on the price of his condo, and I would not know that until my meeting.

My meeting with Paul was very interesting. He was very familiar with my marketing, read my monthly e-newsletters, and saw many of my postcards. Paul had a house with a very unique design and décor. In his kitchen, he replaced the builder-grade engineered wood with reclaimed granary oak, a pricey and very unique type of wood. He took out the original wet bar in the dining room because he did not think he needed a sink so close to the kitchen sink. In the main living room and hallways, he covered the original wood floors with carpet. Most of his furnishings looked like they would be more at home in a college bar than a condo. Essentially, his home looked more like a really awesome bachelor pad than a luxury condo worth more than $1 million.

I knew the appearance would be a challenge, because he spent money making changes and getting furnishings that he enjoyed but that would be viewed as a negative by potential buyers. In order to make my estimate of $1,150,000 valid, I would have to get a stager in his home. During my meeting, I pointed out to him the challenges he would face in selling his home.

First, there was the issue of price. With no comparables available, the only thing to go on was our parallel analysis, which pointed to $1,150,000. He asked me if it would be better to price higher or lower. In most cases, I believed going lower would make sense. With great marketing, a bigger pool of buyers would be driven to see the house. The lower price would create a sense of fear of loss. Buyers would bid more, and the price would be driven up or beyond true market value. I had seen this before, but it was more common in cases where the home being sold is a more commonly available product with more comparable sold homes to analyze. In his case, I thought going higher might make sense since it was a rarely available home. The theory was that since we did not have a good sense of potential value, going higher would set an anchor price in the minds of buyers. Going lower would have the reverse effect. Again, this strategy is one I would only recommend when there are no comparable solds available and the home is a unique or rarely sold type.

The other issue was the appearance. I told Paul that while he might have loved the changes he made to the condo and the furnishings, it would not work for potential buyers who did not share his exact tastes. I recommended a stager who had done great work for another colleague, and he agreed to interview her. We would also have to coordinate a handyman to work with the stager to re-paint some of the walls that were not colors that most buyers would appreciate.

As far as price, Paul wanted to list at $1,250,000. I thought it was high, but within reason, given the strategy for setting a higher anchor price. I told him my plan was to market it as a one-of-a-kind place, which it really was. I would highlight that it was the biggest outdoor space you could find in a condo in the area. In fact, I planned on high-lighting that it was bigger than most backyards of single-family homes in the area. I thought this might attract families and people who wanted outdoor space, as those types of buyers would never normally consider condos. I would also highlight that the developer had origi-nally intended to keep this condo for himself. By marketing it as the "Developer's Suite," I would play more into the uniqueness of it. Fi-nally, I would do a kickoff open house with wine and cheese at night, because this setting would really highlight the nighttime views and how great the condo was for entertaining. These two strategies were designed to attract buyers who had a need to be seen as being signifi-cant.

Paul liked everything he heard and wanted to list his condo with me. His only stipulation was that I pay him a 25% of the commission as a referral fee, since he was a commercial broker. He had mentioned this before, so I was expecting this request and willing to accept. I told him the stager would contact him the next day. I was excited about the opportunity of selling the most expensive condo in the Clarendon Metro stop. I knew that completing this transaction would give me the chance to go into higher-priced homes in nearby areas as well as the chance to meet several potential buyers and sellers in the area.

The next day I came back with Barbara, the stager. She was excited about the opportunity to help with such a unique condo. I reminded her that it would get a lot of good exposure for her and that if she did a great job it would surely lead to more business. After touring Paul's condo, she had numerous recommendations. Paul did not have a din-ing room table, so she wanted to get a really nice glass table to help maintain the openness of the home. Since the living room couch looked like one that belonged in a nightclub, she also recommended renting a different one. Other recommendations included rearranging the patio furniture to showcase the view better, getting new linens, hanging clothes on thin hangers rather than the ones from the dry cleaner, new wall hangings, and more organization in general. Her ad-vice would make the condo look more upscale, more open, and more ready to move in for the average buyer. She gave Paul a quote for $10,000, which was less than 1% of the home value. Although he was hesitant, I explained to him that staging usually cost more than 1% of the home value and that he was under that threshold. I added that staging would definitely reduce his time on market and get him more than a 1% increase on his sales price.

Paul agreed, and the staging effort began. Having been a bachelor pad for several years, it took Barbara a few full days of organizing as well as Paul taking several items away. During this time, one of my normal contractors worked on repainting the dark green accent wall to a more neutral gray as well as touching up several trim pieces and doors. After a few days, the condo was ready for the rental furniture. With the chic glass dining room table and different couch, Paul's living room and dining room had a modern look that should appeal to many high-end buyers. After all of the work, it felt more spacious, more modern, less cluttered, and like a place that many buyers would be able to envision as home.

Paul's condo now looked like one worth well over a million dollars. When the photographer came, I arranged for him to get access to the roof so he could take an aerial photo of the large balcony. The photo would really help to give a good sense of the enormous size of the patio. The photos of the inside came out just as spectacularly, and I was now ready to begin marketing the "Developer's Suite."

For my marketing campaign for Paul's condo, I really tried to increase the cool factor while still playing to the idea that this could be a great place for a family-oriented buyer. I designed a postcard to announce the kickoff happy hour open house, which showcased the patio and had stock photos of a rooftop happy hour. I made a YouTube video that pointed out that the rooftop terrace was bigger than most yards in the nearby single-family home neighborhoods. I pushed this out through all of my social media and Internet channels. Once buyers were in the house, my brochures also highlighted the rooftop patio feature.

The Saturday evening open house went very well, with over two dozen people attending. The views were stunning at night, and I had wine and cheese brought in to help make it a festive atmosphere. One particular older lady stayed the entire time. I was delighted the next day when she requested to come back with her agent. They took another two hours to view the place and later that evening the agent told me her client would be submitting an offer the next day.

I was thrilled at the prospect of getting such a great sale in only three days, but my joy decreased greatly when I received the offer on Monday. Although it was a cash offer with no contingencies, it was only $1 million, a full $250,000 under list price. I knew this was not even close to something that would work with Paul. When I told him, he clearly felt insulted. I told him I understood that feeling and recommended accepting the timeline and cash portion of the offer but countering at the full list price because she was so far off on price. He calmed down and agreed to that.

With only three days on the market, I thought this was the right response to an offer that was 20% under the list price. The buyer did not, and she decided to walk away and focus on other homes.

We decided to keep hosting open houses until the traffic went down. During the next two weekends the open houses drew a lot of traffic, but nobody who was serious enough to talk about an offer. I started to warn Paul, as we got closer to 30 days on the market, that he might want to consider a price reduction. At the time he was hesitant but said he might consider it after 30 days. He also told me if it did not sell within a few months he would also try to rent it out. I certainly did not want him to have to make that choice.

During the fourth open house, an older couple, Mr. and Mrs. Lee, stopped by. They had been out of town for the last three weeks and this was the first chance they had to see Paul's condo. They already lived in the building in a two-bedroom condo, but they were interested in having more room. The third bedroom would make it easier when they had family visit, and the patio would be a great spot for their grandchildren to play.

Mr. and Mrs. Lee were excited about the home and wanted me to come look at their condo and let them know how much it could sell for so they could decide if they wanted to make an offer. After the open house, I researched the comparable sold condos. It appeared that a sales price of $625,000 was probably a very good estimate, but it was possible to get a higher number. I met with them, toured their condo, and went through my typical listing presentation. They owned their condo outright and had some other assets, so if they could sell their home it would be very easy for them to get a very small loan.

They wanted to talk to a loan officer, but telephone calls were a little challenging for them because English was their second language. The next day I arranged for a loan officer who was very familiar with the building to come and meet with them in person. He went over their bank and investment statements and gave them a pre-approval letter contingent upon selling their condo.

Mr. and Mrs. Lee were happy they could purchase Paul's condo if they sold their current one. They decided to list their condo with me and make it effective upon negotiating a deal with Paul. Although I told them that $625,000 was the most likely sales price, they wanted to try to list their home for $650,000. I agreed but told them if they did not get an offer within the first few weeks, they would have to drop to $625,000 or risk losing a potential deal for Paul's place, because a prolonged contingency period might make him lean toward getting out of the deal and renting his place out. They agreed to those terms.

Mr. Lee decided he wanted to write an offer for $1,150,000. He would only have one contingency, the sale of his home. Since he was confident about getting financing as long as he sold his place, he did not feel like he needed a financing contingency. He also did not need an appraisal contingency because his down payment was going to be so big that there would be no risk of his not meeting the lender's loan-to-value requirement. His home-sale contingency would give him 30 days to get his home under contract and a total of 60 days to close on Paul's home. During that time, Paul could still market his home in a status called "contingent with a kickout." This meant that if another buyer came along and wrote an offer without a home-sale contingency, Paul could give them notice and they would have a certain amount of time, in this case three days, to remove the contingency or be replaced by the new buyer.

When I presented the offer to Paul, he was just as unsure about the home-sale contingency as he was about the price. I explained to him that the home-sale contingency actually reduced his risk in this case.

While this is usually not the case, in this scenario it definitely was. Because his condo was more expensive and more rare than most, it was more of a niche product. Mr. and Mrs. Lee were selling a two-bedroom condo that was only slightly above the average condo price. Therefore, it was much more of a commodity product when compared to Paul's condo. There were more condos like Mr. Lee's than like the condo Paul had. There were also a lot more buyers looking for condos like Mr. Lee's. There were also a lot more comparable solds in Mr. Lee's price range, so coming up with an estimate of Mr. Lee's condo was a lot more predictable. All of these factors made it a much safer bet that Mr. Lee would be able to sell his condo quicker than Paul could sell his. This meant that if Paul took this offer he would be transferring the risk of selling his condo (high risk) to the risk of selling Mr. Lee's condo (low risk). When I put it in terms like that the home-sale contingency no longer bothered Paul.

Paul decided to counter Mr. Lee's offer at $1,200,000. At the time he told me that was as low as he would go. Now they were only $50,000 apart and they were halfway there. When I met with Mr. Lee, he was pleased at the counteroffer but wanted to negotiate some more. He decided to counter at $1,180,000, just a little over the halfway mark.

When I took this number back to Paul I was sure he would take it right away. It was less than 6% off his list price, which he had intentionally set high in order to establish a high anchor price for his niche condo product. It would also be the first condo sale in the area for over one million dollars. As long as I could sell Mr. Lee's condo, a much easier task, Paul would get a great sale. To my surprise, he said he would need to think about it for a day. I did not pressure him, but I did remind him that this would be a great number. The next day, after talking to his cousin, who was a real estate agent, Paul called me and told me he was going to take the offer. He was happy with the number.

When I gave Mr. Lee the news, he radiated joy. His grandchildren lived nearby, and he and his wife were excited about the time they would get to spend with them on the outdoor terrace. They were going to get to move into their dream home.

I was thrilled as well. It would be one of the most high-profile sales in the area. I was able to make a buyer and seller happy while getting a great home under contract. It would be a great marketing opportunity. I would now have another listing in the building. I was completely dominating that condo building in a way that no one ever had done in the area. Everyone was happy. There was just one not-so-small order of business left. I had to sell the Lees' condo.

Compared to Paul's condo, I thought selling the Lees' condo would be fairly easy. After all, it was barely half the price, and at $650,000 it was a price point with a lot more buyers. The inventory was not great in that price range, either, so there was even more reason for me to think it would get under contract quickly.

Within three days of getting the contract for Paul's condo, I had the Lees' condo on the market with my full marketing campaign: brochures, direct mail, direct e-mail, phone calls to top open-house prospects, e-mail blasts to real estate agents, and more. During the first open house, I had over a dozen people come. It was a good number of people but not quite as good as the first open house I had at Paul's condo. I also had four agent showings the first weekend on the market. Again, that was a good number but not nearly as good as I had seen on previous listings that year. I was hoping to be in a situation where two days after the open house I was reviewing multiple offers. However, the Monday after the open house it did not appear like I was going to get any offers at all.

Tuesday came and we had nothing. I had called all the agents who showed it and none had clients thinking about writing an offer. When I called all the open-house prospects, I got the same answer. Although the condo was bigger than most two-bedroom condos, people either did not like the layout or did not like the views. It was a corner unit, and one side had great views overlooking the Metro area. The other side looked toward a fire station and an older building. As far as the layout went, a lot of people wanted a kitchen that had more counter and cabinet space.

The next two weekends we got the same results and similar feedback. With 17 days on the market now, I told Mr. Lee it was time to drop their list price to $625,000. The lower price point would bring in a bigger pool of buyers, ones that I hoped were not as picky as the buyers we had seen the first 17 days. We also rearranged the kitchen to make it look roomier and decided to leave the blinds halfway closed on the side of the condo with the less-desired view.

The strategy worked almost immediately. During the next open house, we had twice as much traffic. One person in particular, Michelle, who lived in a one-bedroom condo in the building, really appeared to like the condo, spent an hour looking at it during the open house, and wanted to come back at a later time to see it with her agent. Michelle was renting a one-bedroom condo in the building and thought she could save money and build equity by purchasing a two-bedroom condo and then getting a roommate to pay her rent for the second bedroom.

She decided to write an offer for full price, but wanted a financing and appraisal contingency. Michelle had just started the process and got pre-approved with a lender who was familiar with the building but who was not one of the regular lenders I used. She offered to close within 30 days. While we would have preferred that she use a lender I was more familiar with, everything else about the offer was solid: 20% down payment, 10% earnest money deposit, and a 30-day close. Mr. and Mrs. Lee were thrilled when I presented them the offer, and they accepted. Paul was also very happy when I told him the news. I was on track to sell three transaction sides in the Phoenix building to-taling nearly $3 million in volume. The commission check from this series of transactions would be over $80,000, almost the total of my entire base salary from the previous year. This would also continue to build on my dominance in the building and lead to more marketing opportunities to get market share in nearby buildings. It was a win for everyone.

Michelle seemed to be tracking toward all the milestones along the way in making her purchase. After ratifying the contract, I delivered the condo documents to her, and she did not come up with any objec-tions. Two weeks later, the appraisal came back and it met the required value. Everything was on track, and the only item left was the final approval of the loan.

That is where the trouble began. A few days before the financing contingency deadline, I called buyer's agent and asked if the lender had given final approval for the loan. The agent did not know and did not have any information. Although it is disappointing to hear this, it is an all-too-unfortunate reality of the real estate business. Many agents do a poor job of communicating with lenders, other agents, and even their own clients. This was a huge warning sign. If the buyer did not get approved for the loan, she could get out of the contract without defaulting. This would also allow Mr. and Mrs. Lee to get out of the contract to purchase Paul's condo and then everyone would be set back for weeks and I would potentially lose all of the deals.

Rather than dwell on it or get mad at the agent, I became proactive about finding a solution. I called the lender to get an update directly from him. According to the lender, they were having trouble verifying Michelle's income. Michelle ran a two-person IT company. Although she stated a very large income for her small business, she used several "personal expenses" to reduce her taxable income. While this may be a good choice for many small business owners, lenders look at expenses for self-employed people as expenses needed for running the business, no matter what the reason the owner chose for taking them. Unfortunately, this reduced Michelle's income past the point where the debt-to-income ratio would be high enough for the bank to approve the loan.

I asked the lender what other choices we had, and even threw around a couple of ideas: having her restate her earnings and tax return, getting a cosigner, putting down more money. He said any of these could be a workable solution, so I began to explore ways to do this directly with Michelle. The first option was out because if Michelle restated her earnings and filed an amended tax return, the extra income tax due would prevent her from having enough money for a down payment. The second option might work, and Michelle decided she would ask her mother if she would be willing to cosign on the loan. Michelle could not increase her down payment, because it would take away from reserves she needed for herself and for her business.

After thinking about it for a few days, Michelle's mother decided against cosigning for the loan. Although she knew it was an extremely long shot, she did not want to put her retirement at risk in the event that something went wrong down the road later and Michelle defaulted. I did think that if I could have switched Michelle to the lender

I recommended, he would be able to find a workable solution, but Michelle had lost the desire to move ahead with the purchase. Michelle's agent was somewhat lackluster about the deal as well, even though it was exactly what her client needed. This can often happen when a buyer hits a delay and does not have a strong agent pushing them.

Before I broke the news to the Lees and to Paul that the deal was not going to go through, I came up with an idea. What if I bought Mr. and Mrs. Lee's condo? I thought I would be able to do it with a 10% down payment. If I did that, my total commission on the deal would be just under $100,000 because I would get another 3% commission on the sale of the Lees' condo. At 10% down, I would be investing just over $60,000 to get an additional $100,000 of income. It would be an instant return of 166%, plus I would get to enjoy the benefits of owning a bigger condo, having a bigger tax deduction, and having the future benefits of building up equity. As another benefit, I thought I would be able to market to people that if I could not sell their home, I would buy it, essentially guaranteeing their sale if they were a move-up buyer.

Before discussing this idea, I checked with my lender to make sure I could qualify for the loan. Because I was now self-employed, I needed to make sure the lender could count on my income. The lender said they had one investor who would count year-to-date income for self-employed people if they could get a profit and loss statement that was audited by an accountant. I called the accountant I used the year before for my taxes and asked if this was something he could do. While auditing financials was something that was usually a big job for him, he felt he could do a type of audit that would satisfy the lender's requirements and not be too timely or costly. A one-person real estate agent business usually has fairly simple bookkeeping as long as you have kept up with your financials. Luckily that was something I had done every month.

My accountant quickly came back with a year-to-date profit and loss of $155,000. While this would have been more than enough to qualify if the lender had doubled this six-month period and counted $310,000 in income, unfortunately that was not how the lender decided to calculate the income. Instead, the lender had to count that number for the entire year, effectively reducing my income by half. That put my debt-to-income ratio over the acceptable level. However, it was not over by that much, and if I put down another 5%, for a total of 15%, I would be able to qualify for the loan. I still saw this as a great investment opportunity. My $90,000 down payment would give me an immediate additional income of $100,000, so the return was still fantastic, and it was also a great deal for all of the other reasons I previously mentioned.

I decided to go ahead with my plan to buy the condo. I wrote up an offer with the exact terms of what Michelle had offered, except the lender said he would be able to close in 14 days. That would only put us a week behind the original schedule. I called Mr. and Mrs. Lee and scheduled a meeting with them. When I told them Michelle had not been able to get financing, I could see the huge disappointment in their faces. However, it was quickly replaced with joy when I told them that I would be able to buy their condo on the exact same terms. They were overjoyed that I was stepping in and that they would still be able to get their dream retirement condo. Paul was relieved as well when I gave the news to him. Again, it was a win for everyone involved.

Two weeks later I purchased Mr. and Mrs. Lee's condo. The lender allowed me to have up to 3% of a seller credit, so I took a credit from Mr. and Mrs. Lee for 3% and then reduced the commission I charged by that amount. I used that credit to pay for closing costs, prepay a year of condo dues, and have a contractor make some upgrades to the kitchen and lighting. This made an already great financial situation even better, because I would be able to reduce some of my taxable income while still retaining all of the financial benefit.

The next day Mr. and Mrs. Lee purchased Paul's condo. All were extremely happy and would later become repeat customers as well as refer me to friends and family. I created a ton of value for them and in return I got a ton of value back in the form of a big commission check, a new condo, more local dominance, and new marketing opportunities through a guaranteed sale program that had a real story behind it. The size of these sales also made me the number-one selling agent in the entire ZIP code year-to-date, with only five months left in the year.

Chapter 8:
Pre-Selling to Other Agents

In August my next clients, Darrel and Jamie, contacted me after receiving lots of my direct mail and seeing my open house signs. They lived in a boutique condo building called Clarendon 3131, located just one block from the Phoenix condo. Darrel and Jamie bought their condo two years earlier, when the building was new. Since then, they had a baby and were looking for a bigger place to grow their family.

Before meeting with Darrel and Jamie, I dropped off a pre-listing packet. The packet contained a brochure I had made with a short version of my biography, client testimonials, a description of the types of services I offered, my focus areas, and statistical proof of my performance above the rest of the market. The packet also contained samples of my marketing materials, including direct mail pieces, brochures, and printouts of my e-mail newsletters. I also included a printout of statistics showing my YouTube views, e-mail newsletter click-through rates, and landing page results for properties listed on my website. Finally, I included tips on how to get your house ready for showings and a blank template of a listing agreement. The packet basically included everything I would go over in a listing presentation, with the exception of data for a competitive marketing analysis. I did not want to give away pricing information before I had a chance to meet with Darrel and Jamie and get their commitment.

> **Dan's Tip, Pre-Selling Yourself:** Before you go on a listing appointment, start conditioning the sellers to know and understand the value you bring to the table. Drop off a pre-listing packet. At a minimum, it should include the following: a basic overview of your marketing, a short version of your biography (or your team's biographies), statistical proof of your success in selling (if you do not have any of your own, use team or broker statistics), social proof from previous clients, and a basic questionnaire about the sellers and their house.

When I showed up for my listing appointment with Darrel and Jamie, they were very impressed by everything they had already read about me. I listened to them describe their needs and what they wanted in their next house. They had a baby under ten months old, and both of them worked, so they wanted to avoid a prolonged listing period and having to deal with multiple showings. They also wanted to find a house in an up-and-coming neighborhood that they could afford now but that would be big enough for them as their family grew. The formal part of my listing presentation went fast because the pre-listing packet had made them very familiar with the benefits I could offer them.

Darrel and Jamie decided to sign a listing agreement and buyer agency agreement that night. They felt that they would be flexible in the requirements for their next home, so they were okay with listing their home before finding their next one. They thought it would take about a week to get their home ready and wanted to then have a pre-marketing period of two weeks. That gave them three weeks to look for potential new homes before their house was listed in the MLS. Their condo building was only a few years old, and there had not been a resale yet.

Based on what I had seen other condos in the area sell for, I thought they could get at least $700,000 for their home. It was bigger than most condos, and because it was on the ground level, it had a walk-out terrace big enough to have a grill, which was rare for the area. I thought we could use that rare feature to possibly push the price above $700,000. They thought their home would sell for $700,000 at most but decided to list their home for $725,000. Darrel and Jamie paid $600,000 for their condo with a 3% down FHA loan, so they were thrilled at the potential return on their investment. I was also thrilled to get the first chance to get a resale in a new building in the area.

I began designing their MLS search while Darrel and Jamie got their house ready for the market. I kept the search criteria wide, because I had found that it was better to go slightly wider than needed early in the search and then make refinements later as I got feedback from them on different houses. A few days later we started looking at a few homes and visited five of them. I could tell after the first couple of homes that although they had said they were okay with buying a home that needed updating, they would feel much more comfortable if the home was in move-in-ready condition. While buying a home that needs work can be a great deal, there can also be uncertainty about the time or money needed to get the home in top shape. Many buyers place a value on the certainty of knowing what they are going to get that is greater than the potential value of "sweat" equity.

Based on this realization of their preference, I suggested to Darrel and Jamie that they consider new construction homes or renovated homes in a neighborhood about a mile away. The area was an up-and-coming area that consisted mainly of older homes, but builders were buying older homes in the neighborhood and renovating them or tearing them down and building completely new homes. This process was changing the characteristics of the area and increasing home values. In surrounding neighborhoods, this type of transformation helped buyers who got in early in the process to build up equity. I thought this area would be a good opportunity for Darrel and Jamie.

Not too long after I told them about this, they began to drive around the neighborhood in order to get more familiar with it. After one of their drives, they told me about an older house that was being renovated and had a sign in the front yard that said, "Classic Homes." I looked it up when they gave me the location and found that the builder, Classic Homes, recently bought the property and was in the beginning stages of a complete renovation. Classic Homes was a builder that focused on doing complete renovations. Rather than completely tear down homes, they would maintain the existing foundations and first-level walls on ramblers and then do a renovation that increased the size of the home by expanding it horizontally and/or vertically. This process had several benefits. It allowed Classic Homes to save money because they did not have to do a complete tear-down and pour a completely new foundation. It also saved them time because their permitting stage was shorter, as was the build phase. Instead of taking a year to turn around a new home, they could do it in six months or less. This strategy allowed Classic Homes to sell homes that were nearly completely new and a much better price to the buyers.

I called the listing agent for Classic Homes and got the floorplan for the home they were renovating. When I showed it to Darrel and Jamie they were very interested. It was going to be a two-level home with four bedrooms and three bathrooms on the top level, and a main level with a kitchen, family room, dining room, and another room that could be used as a living room or as a playroom. Everything except for the brick wall on the first level of the home would be brand-new. The home was still in the pre-drywall phase when I showed it to them. To help them get a better idea of what the finished home would look like, I had the listing agent take us to another nearby home that Classic Homes had built. Darrel and Jamie were impressed and were ready to make an offer.

The home would not be ready for another 90 days and was listed at $875,000. At that phase in construction, builders usually did not negotiate too much on price. I showed Darrel and Jamie comparable homes that had sold in the area, but it was challenging to do so because there were not many of them. The homes that sold in that area were typically partially renovated and sold for less, or completely new builds that sold for more. To put it simply, it was hard to find homes to compare this one to for the purposes of determining price. Some of the renovated homes sold for closer to $800,000, but new homes had sold for above $900,000, and a few even above $1 million. This home was somewhere in between, so it was not an exact science as to what the pricing should be. They wanted to offer $825,000 and get the seller to pay for $15,000 of closing costs, which would cover most of the buyer closings costs. I told them there was a good chance we would not even get a counteroffer back at that price—and unfortunately I was right. We made the offer, and Linda, their agent, got back to us rather quickly and told us the builder was not going to negotiate at this point.

Darrel and Jamie were at peace with the response and were ready to get their home on the market. Their home was ready and looked great. I proceeded with my usual pre-marketing strategy and had gotten responses from a few interested buyers. I also got a response from George, an agent in the area who wanted to see it. He saw the YouTube video in an e-mail blast that I sent to area agents and said he had a client who was probably interested. So before I had even put the home in the MLS, I had three interested buyers: two I'd previously met at open houses and one from an agent in the area.

I scheduled all three showings in an hour-long period on the night before I was going to put the home in the MLS. The buyers all knew that the home was not in the MLS yet, so I wanted them to be able to see other people interested in the home so they would have a bit of a fear of loss. I also held the showings very close to when the home would be listed in the MLS, so the buyers knew that many more people would come and see the home if they delayed in their decision to make an offer.

The strategy worked. A few hours after the showings, George called me and told me he was working an offer for my clients and wanted to know terms they were looking for other than price. I told them that because my clients were still looking for their next home, they would prefer closing in 60 days and then having the option to rent for another 60 days after the closing. That would give them four months to find their next home. We received a cash offer a few hours later for $715,000, with zero contingencies and the exact timeline I had requested. I called the other buyers who had seen the home to see if they were interested, but, unfortunately, they were not. When I presented the offer to Darrel and Jamie, they were happy and almost ready to take it. It gave them everything they wanted. They had the security of knowing it would go through because there were no contingencies, it gave them the flexibility to find their next home, and it was $15,000 above the price they thought it would sell for.

Before they decided to take the offer I called George and told him that while my clients really appreciated the offer they were a little nervous about taking something $10,000 below the list price before the open house. George argued that there were no comparables above $700,000 but said he would call his clients to see if they would do anything to make the offer better in order to get it before it hit the market. The next morning I got a call from him and he said his clients would go up another $5,000. Darrel and Jamie decided to take it.

Since they had just got $20,000 more from their house than they really expected even in a best-case scenario, the next week they decided to turn their attention back to the Classic Homes house they wrote an offer on. With the equity they were getting out of their condo, they would have enough money to make a down payment of over 10%. One of the lenders I worked with had a program with no private mortgage insurance (PMI) on 10%-down loans. By eliminating the PMI they had with their FHA loan, getting rid of the condo payment, and having the bigger down payment, Darrel and Jamie's monthly payment did not change much—even if they went up to the full price amount on the Classic Homes house. After seeing a few more homes on the market, they decided they would be comfortable with that home even if they had to pay full price.

After some careful thought and discussions with me, they decided to increase their offer to $845,000 and ask for $15,000 in seller subsidy. This net offer of $830,000 was $45,000 below the list price. When I gave the offer to Linda, I emphasized the value the builder would have in knowing this home was sold so he could begin to focus on acquiring another property for development. Linda came back to me the next day and said the builder would come down to $850,000 and do a subsidy of $10,000. Darrel and Jamie were thrilled, and they were ready to accept the offer.

I called Linda back and told them my clients were happy with the response overall but that they were going to have to come up with a lot of money for the closing and were really hoping for the full $15,000 subsidy. I presented this in such a way that, if it was an absolute deal-breaker for the builder, we could still sign the original counteroffer and get the home while at the same time still ask for another $5,000. Shortly thereafter, Linda got back to me and told me the builder would do the $850,000 price point with the subsidy of $15,000.

Darrel and Jamie were thrilled to get the extra $5,000. They were going to get a brand-new house about a mile away from their condo for a net price of $835,000. They sold their house without ever having to go on the market, which saved them the hassle of keeping their house in showing condition while they were both working and taking care of their baby. After they sold their condo, they were able to rent it back until their next home was ready for them to move in. I delivered them a ton of value on getting their home sold fast, helping them find a new home, and negotiating them extra money on both contracts.

They were extremely thrilled. I was happy as well, not only because of the value I provided them but for having had the chance to get market share in a new building and expand my local presence. Summer was now over and the fall market was about to begin. I was on pace to complete over three transaction sides per month at an average price point of close to $700,000, and my market presence was beginning to grow well beyond the original building I focused on.

Chapter 9:
Using Signs and Finding Inventory on Craigslist

Soon after I got Darrel and Jamie's home under contract, I received a call from Mitch. Mitch and his wife, Sara, lived in Clarendon 3131. They saw how quickly the other place I listed in there went under contract and wanted to meet with me. They saw the sign rider switch from "Coming Soon" to "Under Contract" and were impressed with the speed of the sale. Mitch and Sara lived three floors above Darrel and Jamie's unit. While their home was roughly the same square footage, it had a den in its layout. The other main difference was, of course, the difference of being on a higher level. While this did give them a better view, it also meant that they did not have a ground-level walk- out patio like Darrel and Jamie did. Instead, there was a very small balcony that was big enough for a bistro table and two chairs but not legally big enough for a grill. Based on these things, I thought I would be able to sell it for 1%–2% more than Darrel and Jamie's home, for a total of $730,000 to $740,000.

I delivered my pre-listing packet to Mitch and Sara and met with them the next day. They loved the area and wanted to stay somewhere nearby but wanted to capitalize on the equity they now had in their home and move to a home that would be big enough for them when they decided to start having children. They were impressed with my results for their neighbor and with my presence in the area. They had also seen my signs in other condo buildings and received my direct mail. They were immediately convinced to use me.

The biggest challenge I saw with the situation was the price they thought their home was worth. While Mitch and Sara said they did want to move, they felt like they were not in a rush and wanted to try to get as much money as possible out of their condo, which is a reasonable desire. The problem was with how they wanted to get it. They thought that if they listed their condo at a much higher price, they would have the best shot at getting the most money. While this is a belief that is not too uncommon among sellers, it is one that almost never works and almost always costs people time and money. Homes that are overpriced typically take longer to sell and often sell for less than they would have if they were priced correctly from the beginning. I explained all of this to Mitch and Sara, but they were firm in their belief and wanted to list their home for $775,000, which was $55,000 more than the contract price for Darrel and Jamie's condo. I told them that while we could definitely play up the floor height and having the extra den, the units were similar square footage, and it would be hard to justify such a price increase. Some buyers might actually prefer the lower-level one because of its walk-out patio on the ground level. Even after hearing all of this, they still wanted to shoot for their number. I agreed, but I asked them to agree to a $25,000 price drop after 30 days of being on the market and another $25,000 price drop after 60 days. They agreed, and I got my second listing in the Clarendon 3131 building.

Dan's Tip, Dealing with Overpriced Listings: Although real estate agents give input and recommendations, the choice of a listing price absolutely belongs to the sellers. If a seller wants to list with you but insists on a price that you think is too high, in most cases you should take it. The exception is if the price is extraordinarily high, so high that it would hurt your reputation as an agent and hurt your ability to sell your other listings. If you do take a listing that you think is overpriced, tell the sellers that although you think it is too high, you will do everything to make the case for them. It is critical that they hear your concerns up front. You should also get them to agree to a timeline for price reductions. If the price is too high, doing these two things up front will make it easier later if there are no buyers in sight.

A week later I listed Mitch and Sara's condo. We began the search for their next home at the same time. While they knew they wanted to stay relatively close by, they were not sure about the exact location. In addition to looking at townhomes near Metro stops in Arlington, they also looked at row houses and townhomes in nearby Washington, DC. There were a couple of homes in DC they liked enough to see for a second time, but none of them compelled them to make an offer. They all seemed to missing something in their eyes. They had the same results in the Arlington area.

During the first week of going on the MLS, the interest in Mitch and Sara's condo seemed lukewarm at best. The first open house had close to ten groups come through, but most of them did not seem too interested after considering the price. I got the same feedback from agents who showed the property. However, at the end of the week Mitch and Sara received a cash offer for $750,000. While it was $25,000 under list price, it was $30,000 more than what theirs neighbors had just got. I thought it was a good offer and urged them to take it, but Mitch and Sara wanted to counter at $765,000. When the buyers received the counteroffer, they decided to walk away. Unfortunately, that would be the highest offer Mitch and Sara would receive.

A few more weeks went by and the results were similar, except that as the days on market continued to increase, the traffic decreased—both at open houses and with agent showings. After 30 days on the market, Mitch and Sara dropped their price to $750,000, and the number of showings began to increase.

During this time, I continued showing them houses, but they did not see any that interested them. As their search continued, I not only searched the MLS for homes for them but also looked on websites such as Zillow, FSBO.com, and Craigslist to see if there were any homes not in the MLS that might work. On Craigslist, I came across a townhome in Clarendon Park, the nearby neighborhood where I sold two townhomes earlier in the year. The townhome was going to be listed by the same agent I competed with earlier in the year when I listed Tom and Theresa's townhome. He had apparently learned from my pre-MLS marketing strategy that involved using Craigslist!

Priced at $875,000, the home was in the lower end of Mitch and Sara's range. It was in the same neighborhood where they were already living, but even closer to the area they liked and twice as big as their condo. When I told Mitch and Sara about this townhome, they seemed interested, and we scheduled a showing for the following day.

The townhome was smaller than the two I had sold earlier in the year. Those were two-car garage townhomes, and this one was a one-car garage townhome, which meant the overall width was about eight feet less on each floor. Functionally, it had the same number and type of rooms, but since it was narrower and had less square footage, the market was about $200,000 less, which put this home at a great price range for Mitch and Sara. After seeing it, they were excited about the prospect of living there. Their move would only be three blocks, so they would get to stay in an area they already knew and loved.

After the showing, I called the listing agent to find out more information about the sellers. They were going to list the home in the MLS in a week unless they got an offer before that. They had just had their third child and were building a new house that would be finished in a month. I asked if they would want a rent-back period, and the agent confirmed that the ideal situation for them would be to sell their existing home a week before their new one was finished so they could use those funds for closing and to rent back for a few weeks so they could have a smooth move.

When I talked with Mitch and Sara, this scenario worked for them. Mitch was a doctor, and I was able to find a special lending program for doctors that had low down-payment requirements. They would be able to purchase this particular home with only 5% down. With that level of down payment, they could buy the townhome without selling their existing condo. Since the neighborhood had two townhome sales earlier in the year that were much higher, they were comfortable with not having appraisal or financing contingencies. The only contingency they wanted was a home inspection. I suggested making the home inspection period three days, because that was the length of the HOA document-review period. By making it a three-day period, the home inspection contingency period would add no more additional uncertainty for the seller.

Mitch and Sara decided to offer $850,000 and requested the seller pay $10,000 in closing costs. This was a total of over 4% off the list price, which I knew the sellers would be unlikely to accept before going on the market in a high-demand area. When I presented the offer to the seller, I highlighted that while the offer was not the list price, it did offer the sellers certainty — due to the lack of contingencies — and a relatively stress-free process because the timing would align perfectly with their purchase and move.

The listing agent got back to me later during the day and told me the sellers were happy overall but were countering on price at $865,000 with the subsidy. When I talked with Mitch and Sara, they were happy overall and ready to sign. Before they did that, I told them to let me make one more call to the listing agent. When I called I told that him my clients would come up but that they did not want to come the whole way. I asked him to see what he could do.

About 30 minutes later, the listing agent called me back and told me his clients would do $860,000 with a $10,000 subsidy. My negotiation technique had worked again. By having the conversation verbally I was able to ask for more without rejecting terms that were acceptable to my clients. In this case, it saved them $5,000. Mitch and Sara were thrilled. Now I just had to get their condo under contract in order to make the process less stressful for them.

While Mitch and Sara did not have to sell their condo in order to buy their new townhome, they were not excited about the prospect of having two mortgages. We had just dropped the price by $25,000 to $750,000, and the number of agent showings began to increase that week. The next weekend I marketed the price drop heavily, and the open-house traffic increased, with 15 groups coming through.

I met one couple, Kyle and Alexandra, who both seemed interested. They were a young professional couple who had been renting in the area and looking to buy. They had just begun their search, though, and had not seen many other homes yet. However, they really liked Mitch and Sara's home because the layout was a lot different than many of the smaller two-bedroom condos in the area, which tend to have similar floor plans. The uniqueness of the condo struck them, and I was able to book a follow-up appointment with them for the next day.

During the open house, an agent who had showed the condo a few days earlier came back again with his clients. They had previously seen it in the evening and liked it, but they wanted to come back during the day to see how it looked in daylight. I could tell by their body language and by the questions they asked their agent that they had a lot of interest in the condo.

The next day, while I was showing Kyle and Alexandra the condo, I got a text from the agent who had been at the open house. His clients were going to submit an offer. I told Kyle and Alexandra that if they were serious we needed to discuss crafting an offer. I emphasized that if this was the home they thought they should be in, I did not want to see them miss out without giving it a shot, but if not, I would do everything I could to find them a unique condo in the area that they would love. They told me they appreciated my saying that and that they would get back to me later in the evening after they had a little time to think about it.

A few hours later, Kyle and Alexandra got back to me and told me they decided that they had not seen enough options yet to make a decision. The lender I referred them to had already gotten back to them with a pre-approval and estimates on different types of loan programs. Despite having all of the information, they did not have enough time to think about how much they wanted to spend on their next place, and they wanted to see a few more places before deciding. I thanked them for getting back to me and told them I would follow up with some more options soon.

Meanwhile, I had received the new offer for Mitch and Sara. It came in low. It was $715,000, which was $35,000 lower than their first offer and lower than the contract price of the unit a few floors below them. Mitch was outraged when I presented the offer to him. I understood how he felt, because I knew it must have been tough to hear a number so much lower than the previous offer he received. Real estate is definitely not an efficient market. When you buy stock in a company on one of the major stock indexes, it is the same price around the world. In real estate, a similar property can have a big difference in price in only a matter of days if one property had two interested buyers at the same time and the other one did not. This market inefficiency can produce dramatic differences in results for buyers and sellers. When I explained this to Mitch, it helped him a little, but he was still somewhat in shock from the large swing in the money he was going to get for his condo.

He decided to counter at $740,000. When I took this one back to the buyer's agent, I made sure to tell him that the ground floor unit got $720,000 and this condo had a much better view as well as the extra den. After talking to his client, he came back to me with an offer of $730,000, so now we were only $10,000 apart from having a deal. Mitch and Sara were initially not inclined to go any lower. However, I reminded them that we really did not have any other buyers who were at the point of writing an offer and that if they sat on the market much longer they might have to drop the list price by another $25,000. They decided to send back a counteroffer of $735,000 but wanted me to emphasize this would be their final offer.

When I gave the information to the buyer's agent, he was happy but said he did not know if he would get his client to move up any higher in price. I told him that this was my client's best offer and that they had previously walked away from a higher offer so he should find a way to make it work. A few hours later he got back to me and told me his clients would only come up another $2,500 but said he was willing to make up the difference in his commission. I thought it was a good call on his part. Although he was giving up about 10% of his pay on the deal, the inventory was low and it might take him a while to find something else like this, and one couldn't predict whether his clients would be willing to pay enough at that point as well. Many times buyers can get frustrated during a long search and give up. In any case, Mitch and Sara were happy when I told them the news.

The purchase part of Mitch and Sara's move had been tracking along on time. They did not have any major issues during their home inspection, and the appraisal came back above value. They closed on the townhome a few weeks later and then moved in a couple of days later. They absolutely loved the location and the extra space in their townhome.

A few weeks after that, they sold their condo. For the most part, it went pretty smoothly. There were no issues on the appraisal and the home inspection. There was a minor problem during the final walk-through the day before closing. The buyers claimed that one of the bathroom sinks was draining too slowly. While I did not see this as a material effect that would really be an issue, I did not want it to become a bigger issue than it really had to be. I called one of the contractors I usually worked with and got him to come out and clean out the drain trap. While this cost me $120, it was money well spent because it kept everything on track and everyone happy.

Mitch and Sara ultimately felt happy about the sale of their condo. While it was not as much as their initial offer, it was $15,000 more than the other sale in the building for a unit that was very similar. Furthermore, they really loved living in Clarendon Park. For me it was a great deal, because I gained market share in Clarendon Park and in the Clarendon 3131 condos.

I was now the top agent year-to-date in three of the most popular buildings in one of the area's most popular Metro stops. In fact, that month I became the highest-selling agent of the year in the entire ZIP code. I started to direct mail more of the surrounding condos and townhomes. A few months earlier I had been sending monthly mail to around 1,000 condos and townhomes. Now I had increased that number to 3,000 and in addition to sending "Coming Soon," "Just Listed," and "Sold" postcards, I was sending out monthly price updates for buildings as well as six-pack cards, which were cards that had six of my last sales on them. My presence was growing in the area, and potential buyers and sellers were seeing me in several different ways multiple times a month.

Chapter 10:
Opening More Doors Through Seller Financing

In August and September, while I was selling the condos at Clarendon 3131, I got to put a signpost and large sign outside the building. This was rare for condos, because most of the bigger buildings only allowed small directional signs to be used for weekend open houses. However, because Clarendon 3131 was a small boutique building with a sizable lawn in the front, they allowed more signage. There were many benefits of signage, especially the way I did it.

The signage was a great opportunity to generate buyer leads not only for this seller but for other sellers as well. Many of the agents in the area put brochure boxes out with their signs. I did not do that. I believed putting information out about the house would result in fewer calls. The buyers might see the brochure and think the house would not work for them, or they might see it and not have any unanswered questions. In either case, I would lose a call from a lead, which was a bad thing for everyone. By leaving the information generic, I made my signs act as a sorting mechanism rather than a filter.

For example, if I had a sign out in front of a two-bedroom condo, and the brochure listed the specifications on the home, it is highly unlikely that a buyer looking for a one-bedroom would call me, and vice versa. If someone who was looking for a one-bedroom saw the sign outside of a two-bedroom condo called, I would be able to book them an appointment to see one of my one-bedroom listings. The opposite would be true if someone called me from a sign in front of a one-bedroom condo and was looking for a two-bedroom condo. By leaving this information generic I was able to capture more buyer leads for all of my sellers, which is the advantage of marketing that acts as funnel. If the signs were more specific, they would act like a filter, which would mean fewer leads for all of my sellers. I applied this principle to all of my marketing.

The Clarendon 3131 signs also helped me get phone calls from sellers in the area. One particular seller lived in a townhome across the street. It was a townhome community that was 20 years old. They were smaller than most townhomes in the area but still in a desired location, and they were a great alternative to a two-bedroom condo because they offered more space for the same amount of money. This particular seller, Jon, had accumulated several homes in the area over the previous 15 years. He did not have a super-high income. He was careful about expenses, looked for good deals, and used smart financing. He was the typical millionaire from the book *The Millionaire Next Door*. For several years he had bought properties and rented them out and managed them himself, never missing a chance to save money or cut costs along the way. Six months earlier, he began selling off his properties and had only a few left by the time he met me.

The four-bedroom townhome he contacted me about had four different renters in it. He rented each room out separately. By doing so he was able to get a total of $6,000 in rent, which was about $2,000 more per month than he would have gotten if he rented it out to one family. The renters were under contract for a few more months, but they all wanted to renew their leases again. This made his townhome ideal for investors. Another thing that would be attractive for an investor was seller financing.

Jon told me he did not need the proceeds from the sale and was willing to offer 100% seller financing. He had sold a few of his homes like this before. At the time, 30-year mortgage rates were around 3.5% for buyers looking to move into the home, but they were around 4.0% for investors looking to rent the homes out. Another factor was that banks usually required investors to put down at least 20%, but some times as much as 30%. Jon was willing to do 100% interest-only financing. He would charge 5.0% in interest, but for an investor who did not want to put down a lot of money, the extra percent was a great deal.

Before meeting with Jon, I studied the comparable sold townhomes around his townhome. There were not a lot of similar townhomes that had sold, because it was a very small community. The last sale occurred the previous year and was for $750,000. The market had gone up since then, so I thought $775,000 would be reasonable. When I met with Jon he told me about his situation, what he would offer, and that he wanted to get at least $800,000 for the townhome. He told me he was in no way interested in listing his home with an agent, but would pay me 3% if I brought him a buyer.

I thought it was a good opportunity and did not mind trying to find a buyer for him. I knew there were lots of potential upsides. One was that if it took too long and he did not find a buyer, if I had developed a relationship with him and showed his house to potential buyers, he would be more inclined to use me if he did decide to list his home. Another advantage was that I asked him to refer any buyers he met on his own who were not interested in his home. Jon was happy to do that. Finally, there was also the possibility that I would be able to find him a buyer, get paid a commission, and establish myself in another townhome community in the area.

After my meeting with Jon, I began the search for a buyer. I e-mailed my database of buyers I had met at open houses, which at this point was a few hundred. The headline was, "Rare Chance to Own a Townhome Two Blocks to the Metro with Zero Down Seller Financing." I also posted multiple ads on Craigslist. Some had a similar headline as my e-mail. Others focused on investors, with headlines such as, "Rare Chance to Own a Cash Flow Positive Home with 100% Seller Financing. Tenants in Place!"

Within 24 hours I had three responses to my ads and e-mail. When I called them back to learn more, two buyers were serious, so I booked showings with them. The first showing was with Raymond. Raymond was an investor who owned several properties and was looking to add to his rental portfolio.

To Raymond, the numbers were the most important factor. At $800,000, this place would be great for an investor. The monthly rent was $1,500 per room, for a total of $6,000. After accounting for taxes, condo fees, and maintenance, the net monthly profit was $4,500, or $54,000 per year. Jon was willing to give interest-only seller financing at 5%. That meant the total annual payment would be $40,000. For an investor, this was a great return. An investor could put no money down and make $14,000 a year. The only up-front costs would be taxes and transfer expenses, which totaled $8,000. In just over six months, the cash flow from this investment would be enough for Raymond to recoup his initial costs. Even before accounting for the potential of appreciation, this would be a great investment.

Raymond wasted no time in putting together an offer for the seller's list price. The closing took place in less than a week. Because the seller was providing the financing, the process went a lot quicker and smoother than it would have if a bank or traditional lender was involved. Raymond was happy to have a cash-flowing rental property with almost no money up front or down. Jon was happy, because he sold his home at a great price and now owned a loan that paid him 5%, which was a lot more than he could get from any other type of loan investment. It was a great deal for me because I closed a deal for a client and because Jon let me market the property as sold, which gave me the chance to put another sign up in a Clarendon townhome community and market it via direct mail and online, which increased my presence even more.

The only downside was that Raymond bought the property before I could even show it to the second buyer who inquired about the home. Drew had also contacted me but was out of town for a few days, so he missed out on Jon's townhome. I knew Jon might have some more properties he wanted to sell, so I asked him and he told me he actually had a condo in a town nearby that he wanted to sell. It was a two-bedroom condo that rented for $2,000 that he was trying to sell for $350,000. He offered me the same commission deal if I brought him a buyer, so I scheduled a showing for Drew.

This condo had the potential for instant cash flow under the terms Jon was offering. Jon was offering 5% interest-only financing, which meant the monthly payment would be $1,450. The condo fee was $150 a month and taxes came out to roughly $200 a month, bringing the total monthly expenses to $1,800, which meant the condo would bring in $200 of profit every month. This was a great number for a home that was 100% financed.

Drew decided to take the offer, and everything looked great up until the point that Jon ran a credit check. Jon's terms gave him the right to cancel the sale if the buyer did not meet specific credit criteria. Unfortunately, Drew had a less-than-stellar credit report and several late payments on his rent. Jon was not going to take the risk and canceled the contract.

Rather than get upset, I saw this as an opportunity. I asked Jon if he would substitute me into the contract. Jon agreed. I was still going to get the 3% commission, which made this an even better deal for me. I used the commission as a credit to pay the transfer tax and closing costs and still had nearly 2% left over. I used that money to prepay taxes and condo fees, which would greatly improve my cash flow for the first year. Now I was going to buy the condo with nothing down, no closing costs, and a cash flow of $550 a month for the first year. It was an amazing deal for me that not only gave me a great investment property but also helped me get market presence in another area. A year and a half later I actually sold the condo to another investor and made $30,000 net profit on the sale, an incredible number considering the fact that I put nothing down.

My experience with Jon's condo not only reinforced the importance of leveraging sign opportunities to me but also served as an example of the importance of considering non-traditional methods in real estate. Many agents shy away from things they do not know instead of appreciating the opportunity to learn and grow. I had to learn how seller financing worked and more ways to help owners who did not want to list their homes.

Jon was an example of what a person making an average income could accomplish through careful investing in real estate. Jon's sale taught me the value of doing things outside my comfort zone and offering something that no one else could. Most sellers have a big mortgage, so they're not in a position to offer seller financing. Many buyers, especially investors, like seller financing because it usually has more flexibility than conventional bank options. Since it is rare, but desirable, sellers offering this type of financing can command higher prices in the market. Buying my second listing gave me another example to show sellers how I could guarantee the sale of their home. By marketing guaranteed sales by buying the home if I didn't sell it, I acquired more move-up buyers and charged higher commissions. All this growth required me to get out of my comfort zone and try new things, such as offering commission guarantees or guaranteeing home sales.

Chapter 11:
Getting Buyers to Beat Other Buyers to Listings

With two months to go, I was about to break $20 million in sales on the year. If I kept it up for the last two months, I would go from rookie agent to top agent in my ZIP code in one year. My next clients were Brett and Amy, a couple I had met earlier in the year at an open house in the Phoenix condo. They were renting a one-bedroom condo and wanted more room. They had met me at a two-bedroom condo open house, and while they would have loved the room it had, they believed it was out of their price range. I knew that a one-bedroom plus den condo would be the perfect solution for them, because they would get a lot more room than a one-bedroom condo but would pay $100,000 less than the two-bedroom condo price and have a lower condo fee.

The problem was that at the time there were no one-bedroom plus den condos on the market. I told them about the buyers I helped earlier in the year who bought a one-bedroom plus den condo. I stressed how acting quickly when the condo came on the market helped the buyers beat out other buyers and save thousands of dollars. I also told them that I would take an active role in trying to find condos for them before they came on the market, and I gave them examples of how I had done that earlier in the year for other buyers. They had seen my signs during several of my open houses in the building, so they were very aware of my presence there.

Brett and Amy gave me all of their contact information and told me to follow up with them. A few days later, a one-bedroom plus den condo came on the market in a nearby condo building called Clarendon 1021. I called Brett and Amy and described the condo to Brett. He told me they were interested in seeing it. I wanted to get their full commitment to work with me, so I asked if we could schedule a time to grab coffee, talk for a few minutes, and then see the condo. We scheduled a time to meet that evening.

During my meeting with Brett and Amy, I learned a little bit more about their search. They were first-time homebuyers and did not know much about the process. I went through my buyer presentation and spent much of the time teaching them all about how purchasing works. This included getting pre-approved by a good-quality lender, researching comparable sales in the neighborhood, ways to improve an offer to a seller without raising the price, and what to expect after going under contract.

I also spent some time with them going over financing. They had not contacted a lender yet, so they did not know how much they could get approved for and what payments would look like at different levels. I gave them basic overviews of a few different financing options and gave them the contact information for two lenders. When we were finished, I asked them to sign a buyer broker agreement and they did.

We went to see the new condo that just came on the market, and I could tell fairly quickly that it would not work out for them. They did not like the lighting or the view. This condo was a first-floor condo and did not get a lot of natural light. Right away they were concerned with not only the view and the light but the level of noise from the street. I asked them if they would buy the condo if it were not for the view and the level. They said they definitely would, because the amount of space was perfect and they were already accustomed to the type of finishes (flooring, cabinets, countertops, etc.) it had.

I followed up the following day with Brett and Amy and confirmed they still felt the same way about the view and level of the condo after having a night to sleep on it. Brett confirmed that they did. I also asked about the progress they had with the lenders I recommended. He told me they had spoken with both lenders and submitted online applications. They had already received pre-approval and estimates for different types of loan programs. Based on the estimates they received, they were comfortable with a purchase up to $500,000, which was actually in line with what they thought initially. This was right in the range of what one-bedroom plus den condos in the area cost, so I now knew what I needed to do. I needed to find a one-bedroom plus den condo for them.

Dan's Tip, Help Your Clients Narrow Their Choices: It is important to ask closing and narrowing questions, even if you know the buyers do not want a particular place. Doing so helps you find out what is most important for them to have, or to not have, in the next place they buy. A few more examples of these types of questions are:

Is there anything other than the location on the busy street that would prevent you from buying this home?

Is there anything other than the size of the yard that would prevent you from buying this home?

If this home had a fourth bedroom, would you buy it, or is there anything else that is preventing you from buying it?

These types of questions will help you find out the deal-breakers and priorities of your buyers, and they will make the home search more efficient and less frustrating for everyone.

The low-inventory environment made what would normally be a very simple search into one that presented a challenge. However, these challenging situations are not only opportunities to grow but chances to show your value to your clients. I used the tax records to identify the condos that would work for them in the three buildings they liked. There were about 50 potential targets that I thought might work for them. I typed out a note that said the following:

Dear Homeowner,

I am a local real estate agent with a lot of recent experience in your area. Right now I am working with some buyers who are looking for a condo just like yours. They are pre-approved and ready to buy. Their challenge is that the current inventory is low, and there are no other condos on the market like yours. Due to the low inventory and low interest rates, prices have gone up. My clients are positioned to make an offer with very few contingencies and a flexible closing timeline. If you are thinking about selling at all, please contact me.

Best,

Dan

I spent a couple of hours one evening delivering this note by sliding it under doors in an unmarked envelope along with my business card. In the past, I noticed that doing this was the best way to get responses. I had success with it in nearby condos and townhomes. If the envelope was unmarked and put on or under their door, people were a lot more likely to read it than something that looked like junk mail in their mailbox.

However, this time it did not work. Whether it was the time of year, the smaller size of the number of available homes, or just bad luck, I did not get any responses. It certainly did not get me discouraged, though. Past successes had taught me that you had to be committed and consistent when it came to marketing. Too many agents try something once or twice, or for a few months, and then quit right before it would have been successful.

Although I did not get a response to this marketing attempt, I kept looking for ways to find a one-bedroom plus den condo for Brett and Amy. Finally, I had a breakthrough. I asked the front desk manager at the Phoenix condo building a week later if she knew of anyone who might be moving out. She told me someone on the seventh floor had just scheduled the freight elevator for a move-out and gave me the unit number. It was someone who lived in a one-bedroom plus den floorplan. Even better, it was on the seventh floor, so it had a good view and got a lot of natural light. I immediately put a handwritten note under their door.

I received a call the next day from a Redfin agent. He told me his clients received the note and contacted him about it. He was their listing agent, and they were preparing to put their home on the market. Their hope was to move out in a few weeks and then get their condo repainted and then put on the market. They were going to list it for $480,000. I was a little surprised at the price, because the last one sold for more than this.

I told the agent that I had some very interested clients and if they could see it now they might be willing to write an offer and close quickly, which would save his clients the money and cost of the home being empty. I also told him that I had closed several units in the building that year and so had the lender that Brett and Amy were using. The agent seemed interested in a quick sale and told me he would talk to his clients to see if they would consider a pre-sale.

The agent called me back a few hours later and told me his clients would be willing to show their home before going on the market. I scheduled something for Brett and Amy the next day. When they walked in, I could tell they were going to really like it. They enjoyed the view and appreciated all of the natural light. The floor plan was perfect for them. The only negative item was that it needed a new paint job, but I had already told Brett and Amy that prior to the showing and even gave them an estimate. By doing that, I removed a potential objection before it became a real issue for them.

Brett and Amy told me they wanted to put an offer on the place at list price. I told them everything I knew about the sellers, and we talked about how to tailor the offer to meet their needs. They decided to do a three-week close so the sellers would have minimal vacancy time. Because the condo was clearly priced within the market range, they were comfortable without an appraisal contingency. The lender had a great track record of closing loans in the building and had already approved them for the loan, so they were also comfortable forgoing a financing contingency. The only contingency they decided to have would be a three-day home inspection contingency, which would coincide with the three-day period they would have to review the condo documents. Overall, their offer added no additional risk or uncertainty to the sellers with contingencies, and the timing was exactly what the sellers needed.

After I presented the offer to the listing agent, we received an answer back very quickly that the sellers were going to take the offer. They were happy to get the list price and to not have to worry about the sale anymore. The listing agent was happy for the quick sale. The buyers were happy that they would be able to get the condo for the list price and avoid a potential bidding war. I felt like I delivered great value to everyone involved and that it was another win–win situation.

The home inspection and appraisal went fine. In a few weeks, Brett and Amy closed on their home. I continued to expand my presence in condos in that building and surrounding areas and kept doing it in different ways. In this case, it was the combination of having a good relationship with someone in the area (the building desk manager) who knew when people were moving, and communicating directly with likely sellers in order to help buyers find hard-to-get real estate in a low-inventory market. With one month to go in my first year, I had broken the $20 million mark in sales, an accomplishment achieved by less than one percent of all real estate agents in the county and a mark that only the most seasoned real estate agents usually top.

Chapter 12:
Getting the Best Deals in New Construction

I was determined to finish the year strong and hold my position as the top real estate agent in my ZIP code. Ever since Kyle and Alexandra passed on the condo at Clarendon 3131, I maintained regular contact with them. I set them up on an auto MLS search for all the condos around the Clarendon Metro stop and the adjacent areas. Whenever something came up that I thought would be of particular interest, I would also call them. Regardless of what came on the market, I would also call them at least every week to check in and see how they were feeling about their search.

About a month after I first met them at Clarendon 3131, a two-bedroom condo came on the market nearby that I thought they would like. It was in the Station Square building and was only two blocks away from the Metro. I thought it would be appealing because it had loft-style features. It was not a true loft condo in the sense that it did not have stairs going up to another exposed level, but it did have higher ceilings, larger windows, and exposed ductwork and piping. I thought it would appeal to them because it was in the location they liked and did not have the somewhat cookie-cutter feel they were trying to avoid.

When I called them and told them about it, they were excited to see it. It was priced at $650,000, so it was in the range they were looking for and in the area they wanted as well. That evening I showed Kyle and Alexandra the condo. While they liked it better than some of the other places they had seen, it was not compelling enough for them to want to make an offer. They wanted something more unique and newer. I probed further and asked what would make them feel differently. I asked if they needed a second bedroom. They said it was preferable but that they could be fine with a place with an extra den or work area and did not necessarily need a complete second bedroom.

Based on this conversation, I thought of a place that would be perfect for them. The first phase of a new condo development, called Gaslight Square, had just been built and was only two Metro stops away.

I had not thought of this building for them before because two-bed-room condos there started in the mid $800,000 price range, and I did not think they wanted to go that high. However, now that I knew a one-bedroom condo with an extra den might work, it made this build-ing a possibility. The building had one-bedroom condos that had a loft area with a den. These condos were true loft styles in that they had spiral stairs going from the main living area to the loft and den/bed-room. This design created 20-ft. high ceilings and huge windows in the main living room. There were also two outdoor spaces. Overall, the design was very unique and not like any other condo in the area.

When I took Kyle and Alexandra to see this new building, they absolutely loved it. It had the "Wow!" factor they wanted. At the time, there were two units available there that they liked. Both were similar layouts but with different finishes. They were both priced at $725,000. I had already developed a great relationship with the sales manager and showed the building to several other buyers, so she knew I would continue to bring buyers there and was inclined to give a great deal to anyone I was representing.

However, before Kyle and Alexandra made an offer, there was one more test the building had to pass. They had a large dog, and they wanted to see if he could make it up and down the spiral stairs.

Dan's Tip, How Buyers Get the Best Deal on New Construction: This is a key concept to not only understand but communicate to clients. Many buyers think they can get the best possible deal by going straight to the builder or the builder's sales rep/manager and cutting out the buyer agent. However, this is not the case. Walk-in traffic to them represents one possible sale, but a sales agent represents several possible sales. Therefore, builders and developers are more motivated to give the best deals to the buyers who use good sales agents. There are other ways agents can provide value to buyers in new construction deals (contract review and pricing analysis, for example), but the biggest value is usually in the agent's ability to get them the best possible deal.

The sales manager and I waited while they went to get their dog. During that time I made it a point to let her know more about my busi-ness and that during the last year I had become one of the top-selling agents in the area.

I told her a little bit about where many of my clients came from and let her know that if I was able to get the best possible deal for Kyle and Alexandra, I would make sure to bring any potential clients I had to see the development.

Kyle and Alexandra returned with their dog, and we went back into the home they were considering. Kyle and I and the dog waited in the living room while Alexandra walked up the stairs to the loft area. Kyle took the dog off his leash as Alexandra called for him. I watched as the 80-pound dog easily made his way up the spiral stairs. With the final test out of the way, they were ready to talk about making an offer. I asked the sales manager for their contract and went to a nearby coffee shop with Kyle and Alexandra.

We reviewed the last several units that had closed in the building. The developer had not been negotiating on price but had been paying up to 1% in closing costs, which in this case would have been a little over $7,000. I told Kyle and Alexandra they should try to get more but to be ready if the developer was only willing to go down 1%. I thought asking for up to 4% would make sense, but they should do this in ways other than the price. Developers are often willing to give money through closing costs, upgrades, and other ways than the price. This way, when the property closes and the tax records are updated, the net price appears higher. This helps them get higher prices in future sales.

I had this in mind when I sat down with Kyle and Alexandra to prepare their offer. They wanted to ask for 4% off the list price, even though most of the units had been going for 1% off the list price. I told them that if they wanted to maximize the concessions from the seller they should offer full price but ask for 3% of the closing costs to be paid for by the seller and ask the seller to also prepay their condo fees for two years. This would be a total net back to them of roughly $30,000, which was right around 4%.

When I presented this offer to the sales manager, I reminded her that the full price closing would help sell future units and that if I knew I got the best possible deal, I would be more inclined to bring future clients.

We heard back the next day from the seller. The builder countered the offer with 3% in closing-cost subsidy and one year of prepaid condo fees. This totaled roughly $25,000, which was about 3.5% off the list price. Kyle and Alexandra gladly accepted the offer. Their net price of $725,000 ended up being the best price for any buyer in the building. I helped three other buyers buy homes in the building in the next two months, and they all got unbelievable deals. It was a win–win for everyone involved.

During the same month that Kyle and Alexandra went under contract, I had met Rod and Samantha. Rod and Samantha had recently gotten married and moved in together in the one-bedroom condo in the Phoenix condo that Samantha had owned and lived in for several years. They were interested in getting more space. I had met Samantha before at open houses in the building and talked with her from time to time in the lobby or gym. She and Rod had both seen my marketing postcards as well.

When they called me to tell me they were going to move, they had already picked out where they wanted to move next. Rod and Samantha had decided on a new community of townhomes in the nearby city of Alexandria. The development was being built by a national homebuilder and would have over 500 new residences by the time it was complete. Rod and Samantha had already visited the sales center and picked out the model they wanted.

They initially contacted me because they wanted help renting their condo. When I started talking to them about the rental market, I learned they had already decided on a townhome they wanted to write an offer on. Like the condo at Gaslight Square, I knew I would be more successful in getting them money if I found ways to do it that did not involve the sales price. At $750,000, the townhome was a great deal for the area. Because they were buying in an early phase of development, prices were lower. By the time the developer was finished, the same townhome would go for $900,000.

Instead of asking for money off the list price, we focused on closing cost help and free upgrades. The developer agreed to give them $40,000 in free upgrades plus another $10,000 if they used the company's preferred lender. Rod and Samantha agreed and would close in the next 40 days. I came up with a plan to lease their condo and minimize the vacancy period.

Even though they were under contract, I did not stop trying to find them ways to save money. According to the contract, in order to get the extra $10,000 in closing credits they had to use the Pulte lender. I asked them to get a good-faith estimate, and when they did, the first thing I noticed was that the lender was going to charge them a two-point origination charge. That was just over $15,000. So the builder was going to give them a $10,000 credit, but then the builder's lender was going to charge them an extra $15,000. They were basically giving them a little bit with the left hand and then taking away more with the right hand.

I put Rod and Samantha in touch with a lender I had worked with several times. He gave them an estimate at the same interest rate, with $16,000 less in closing costs. Even though they would have to give up the $10,000 credit from the builder, they would still come out $6,000 ahead because of all the money they would save in loan costs. They were happy that I was able to save them $6,000, but it did not stop there. I told them to send the other lender's estimate to the Pulte lender. When they did, all of a sudden the Pulte lender came back with an estimate at the same interest rate but without the origination charges. They lowered their fees by $15,000. Rod and Samantha decided to go with that loan because they would retain the builder credit of $10,000. They were thrilled that I saved them over $15,000.

Within a few weeks I found a tenant to move into their condo the same week they closed on their new townhome. I minimized their vacancy to almost no time at all. Even though they did not contact me until they had almost finalized their choice of home, I was still able to provide them with massive value, saving them over $15,000 in lender fees, helping them negotiate the biggest credit possible from the builder, and minimizing the vacancy period in their current home, which they were going to convert to a rental. Getting these two new construction sales done was a great way to end the year. It gave me a total of 37 transaction sides for the year and over $22 million in sales. I was the top agent in my target market and was determined to continuing to grow both the breadth and depth of my market share.

Chapter 13:
Concluding Thoughts

In less than one year I became the top real estate agent in my market, surpassing agents who had been in the market for decades. The Appendix contains a list of 100 different possible techniques and tools to use in rapidly growing your business and providing more value to your clients. Many of these techniques helped me grow my business at a hyperfast speed. Whether you are just starting out, have a large established team, or are somewhere in between, I am sure you will be able to find tools there that will be able to grow your business. In this chapter, I will review a few overarching principles that I believe are critical in becoming a hyperlocal, hyperfast real estate agent. In the Epilogue after this chapter, I discuss what has happened since my first year and how I have grown from a single agent model into a team business.

One of the frameworks that I believe help explain my success and can serve as a guide for others looking to start in the business or expand their existing business is the STP framework I discussed earlier in the book. As a reminder, STP is a common business-school and marketing term that stands for (1) segmenting, (2) targeting, and (3) positioning.

1. **Segment your market.** This involves deciding how you are going to divide the market. There are many ways to segment real estate markets. Examples are:

    - Geographic region
    - Price point
    - Profession
    - Social circles
    - People you know (sphere of influence) vs. people you do not know
    - Demographics

In my case I decided to segment the market based on geography. While I think geography segmentation strategy is one of the simplest and easiest ones to execute, other segmentation strategies might be more appropriate for your situation. One key part of segmentation is to make sure you pick the right size segments. It will be easier to gain market share in smaller segments. Larger segments will have more possible transactions. Your experience, marketing budget, and people resources will dictate how large of a segment you can realistically go after.

2. **Targeting is simply picking which segment you are going to go after for your business.** For example, if you choose to segment the market based on price point, you could target lower price points, the median price point, or higher price points. In my case, I decided to segment the market based on geography and targeted homes that were close to a particular Metro stop. Initially, my focus was even narrower, as I targeted homes in one particular condo building. When picking your target, there are several questions about the target market you need to answer. How many homes are in the target market? What is the turnover rate? What is the competition like? Are there a few dominant agents? Are there several dominant agents or is the market totally fragmented? What is the average price point? These questions will help you decide which market is the best to target and how to develop your strategy to do so.

3. **Positioning yourself means how you present yourself in order to attract the people you are targeting.** My business grew rapidly because of two key principles of targeting that I followed. First, I found ways to provide massive value to my clients in an ethical way that was unique, and second, I communicated those results to the people in my market.

The ways I provided value to buyers and sellers included the following:

- Helping clients sell their home off the market in situations where, due to the nature of their purpose for selling, they wanted to minimize public exposure and have a quick, semi-private sale.
- Getting clients a sale at a high number when it was hard to provide a valuation due to low turnover in the market.
- Helping clients minimize the time that they owned two homes during a move-up buyer situation.
- Negotiating low-appraisal situations successfully.
- Getting sellers a better result than the current neighborhood expert.
- Selling homes before they hit the market from my current listings in the buildings.
- Helping sellers get their homes ready for the market and ensuring the homes stayed in top showing shape.
- Buying a home to ensure the sale of another home.
- Finding buyers who wanted seller-financing deals.
- Using my network of agents to sell homes before they went on the market.
- Helping buyers get homes before they went on the market so they could avoid competition.
- Helping buyers win in competitive bidding wars without being the highest-priced offer.
- Getting clients the best possible deal from builders in new construction projects.

Providing clients with massive value is only one part of the equation. It is critical to communicate the value you can provide to your target audience. You must get your message out in a variety of ways. Consistency in your communications is the key. The time to send out direct mail, e-mail campaigns, and social media blasts is now. These are just a few examples of ways to communicate your value to potential clients. You must figure out what will work best for your target audience. You must do it early and frequently, and you must not give up. Too many agents quit a marketing campaign after a couple of months, and most of the time they are likely stopping their efforts right before they are about to produce results.

So we know it is important to segment your market, decide what part of it you will target, and position yourself as best served to provide value to that segment of the market. You must figure out how to provide more value than anyone else and communicate that message to the market consistently, concisely, and clearly. Is there anything else? Yes, there is one more critical element that might be more important than anything else. You must believe in yourself and believe that you will be successful for yourself and your clients. Visualizing success and believing that it will happen—no matter what—is critical. It is like a muscle in that the more you exercise it, the stronger it will be and the more you will be able to call on it in tough situations.

Along with visualizing success, there is another important concept to implement. Although some people in sales might say "Always Be Closing," I believe you must "Always Be Learning." Being a dedicated lifelong learner will increase the number of tools you will have at your disposal. When you learn something new you might not realize when you will call upon that new tidbit of knowledge, but the more you learn the better chance you will have of recalling something that will help when a new challenge arrives. Coaches, seminars, and books are all great resources. You can also learn from every new person or lead you come in contact with and every marketing piece you design or implement. Look outside the real estate industry as well to see what you can learn from leaders in other industries.

I looked at every new prospect as a chance to learn and grow as well as a chance to strengthen my ability to visualize. Whenever I met with new prospects, I always believed I would be able to provide them with the most value and that I would be able to convince them to work with me. If I did not succeed, I was letting myself and them down, because they would not be getting the best possible service available. The more you are able to adopt that mind-set, the stronger you will be when you are rejected. There were several times throughout my first year (and even more since then) when I was initially rejected. Sometimes I was rejected several times, but I always believed that it was temporary and that I would eventually win them over. More often than not, I did win them over. So my final message is to always believe in yourself, set big goals, and never give up.

Don't be a stranger! One of my favorite things about the real estate business is the opportunity to teach and learn from other agents, and share our successes with each other.

Connect with me on Facebook, Twitter, Instagram and LinkedIn to post a review, tell us your success story, and share some advice of your own!

Facebook: www.facebook.com/thedanlesniak
Twitter: twitter.com/thedanlesniak
Instagram: instagram.com/thedanlesniak
LinkedIn: linkedin.com/in/danlesniak/

As a bonus, if you post a picture of yourself with this book and include #HyperFastAgent in the caption, I'll give you a free download of my 100 Tips and Strategies to Grow Your Business and Provide More Value to Clients!

Epilogue

The hyperlocal, hyperfast real estate strategy has continued to work, and during the five years since I began to use it my business has continued to grow and evolve. While I believe rapid growth is important, I believe sustained success is even more important because it is a sign that you are conducting your business ethically and in a way that adds value to your clients. If you do not conduct your business ethically and provide value to your clients, it will be difficult—if not close to impossible—to have sustained success. I believe this is true not only in real estate but in any business.

In order to add massive value to clients in the real estate industry, you have to be talented in several different areas, including, marketing, negotiating, administration, finance, accounting, and psychology. Although it is rare for one person to have expertise in all of these areas, the best solo agents do. If there is an area in which you are lacking technical expertise, you either need to hire someone to fill that gap or rapidly become an expert in it yourself by reading books, going to seminars, finding a mentor, or doing whatever it takes.

The one resource that everyone is equal in is *time*. You and I have the same amount of it. Bill Gates, Warren Buffett, and Mark Zuckerberg do not have any more time than you and I do. Although different people have different levels of efficiency with time, everyone has the same finite amount of it. There are just 24 hours in a day.

So how does the time constraint affect your real estate business? Even if you are technically proficient at all the functional areas in real estate, at some point—if you want to grow your business—time will constrain you to a point where you will see the wisdom of hiring one or more people to help you. Growing bigger, in a smart way, will allow you to add even more value to your clients. First, as your market share grows, you and your team will become better at knowing the market. An agent who does 30 transactions a year will know the market better than an agent who does five transactions a year. A team that does 100 transaction a year will know the market better than an agent who does 30 transactions a year. Second, you will be able to pour more resources into developing systems to better serve your clients. There are count-less examples of solo agents who are successful but are afraid to hire help even after they reach their time-constraint limit. Solo agents can-not develop systems to acquire and serve clients as well at team can. Finally, you will have more resources to put back into marketing, which will help your sellers find buyers and your buyers find homes.

After 37 transactions in my first year, I knew I had to start hiring other people if I wanted to grow. At the end of my first year, I hired an assistant. Not long after that, I hired an agent to help me with my buyer leads. A few months later, I hired two more agents and a mar-keting assistant. I rapidly made the transition from a solo agent to a team leader.

During this transition period, I met my future wife, Keri Shull. At the time, Keri was a competitor who led the Keri Shull Team (kerishull.com), which focused on new construction homes in Arling-ton. In a short period of time we dated, fell in love, got married, and combined our teams. This led to even more hyperfast growth, and in 2013 we did nearly 150 transactions and became the biggest team in the entire Arlington market. We continued to apply the STP frame-work, and we expanded into new parts of the market and deepened our presence where we already had market share. In 2014 we com-pleted nearly 250 transactions and formed our own brokerage, Optime Realty, which is home to the Orange Line Living (livetheorange-line.com) and Keri Shull Team brands. In 2015 we completed 370 transactions for a total of over $225 million in sales, making us the number-one selling real estate team in all of Virginia and one of the top 50 in the United States. Our team has now grown to over 30 people, and as we get bigger we continue to find new ways to add value to our clients and new markets to enter. The agents on our team average net annual incomes of over $120,000, levels that are unprecedented in the industry. What makes this even more remarkable is that most of them are doing it with very little real estate experience. We have also en-tered other functional areas, including real estate development, which has given us the opportunity to help several families build their dream homes. Today we continue to enjoy setting new goals, growing bigger in all area of our lives, and providing more value to those around us.

Appendix
100 Tips and Strategies to Grow Your Business and Provide More Value to Clients

I often hear agents say they have tried everything but cannot seem to find a way to have success. When I hear this, I always ask what specific things have they tried? Rarely do I get a list longer than a couple of items, and usually they try something once, twice, or a few times at most before deciding that it does not work. Often they give up right before the breakthrough was about to occur. There are several different ways to break into a new target market or expand and grow your established one. I put together a list of 100 methods that I have seen work. While this is nowhere near an exhaustive list, it is definitely one you should try to complete before declaring that you have tried everything and nothing works. You should also realize that while these methods are likely to help grow your business hyperfast, you cannot just try them once or twice. Consistency is the key.

SEGMENTATION, TARGETING, POSITIONING

1. Figure out how you are going to segment the market and then pick the segment that you are going to target. It could be a geographic area, a group of people you know, or people in a certain type of industry. Position yourself to this segment as the best person to deliver the most value. If you are already established in the industry, this can also work as a way to grow your business or expand it to a new area and reduce your overall business risk.

2. You must have the mind-set that you will break into your target segment. Make it something that is a must for you and that you will not compromise on.

3. Market to your target area through several different channels, including the following: social media, your website and/or blog, direct mail, signs, and e-mail.

4. Create or get an e-mail list of your targets and e-mail them on a regular basis. Condo buildings usually have e-mail lists to communicate with owners. If you are an owner in a building you are targeting, or know owners, ask them and you might be able to get a list. Sometimes they are easy to get. Sometimes all it takes is someone accidentally using CC instead of BC on an e-mail message. Another way is to collect e-mails at open houses when people sign in. That will build you a targeted list of buyers interested in the area. In any case, the time to build your targeted lists is now. I have several, and I e-mail them at least once a month.

5. Always keep your head up and your eyes and ears open, especially in your target area. You never know when you will get a piece of information that might help you find a client. As I mentioned in the text of the book, one time I saw a photographer taking pictures in a condo building's common areas and asked him what home he was going in to take pictures of. I put up an ad on Craigslist stating that a great condo was "Coming Soon." A buyer contacted me about it and decided to use me as her agent and ended up buying that condo a few days later.

6. If you find a good deal on a home and it is not on the market yet, do not be afraid to buy it yourself, especially if it is in your target area. If it is a good rental or flip investment, take it. You are getting not only a great deal but also more marketing opportunities and more presence in your target market.

ADDING VALUE

7. Find a way to add more value to your target segment than anyone else. If you are experienced, it might be your track record of success, marketing advantages, or the size and experience of your team or staff. If you are new, it might be the useful experience you have in another industry, your complete focus on just a handful of clients, or the fresh ideas you can bring to the table. Different things will work for different markets, but it is imperative that you not only find out how to deliver more value than others in your

target market but also communicate this fact at a broad level and a personal level.

8. It is important to establish relationships with good contractors. They will usually give you and your clients great service, good response times, and good prices. You can create value through these referrals, and they are especially helpful during tough negotiations, when getting the best possible price is very important.

9. Don't stop looking for ways to save your clients money after the contract is ratified. See if there is a better loan program for them, better contractor, cheaper moving company, and so forth. Become the expert on the entire process and save them money and time at each step of the process. The more value you create for them, the better the experience and the more referrals you will get.

10. Create risk-mitigation strategies for move-up buyers. When buyers must sell their current home to buy their next home, it makes the process more difficult but gives you a chance to add even more value. One way to do this is to give them a guaranteed price. If buyers are buying a home through you and need to sell their home, give them a guaranteed price that you will buy it at. If the home does not sell, you will have three commission sides (the buy side of the home they are buying and the buy and sell sides of the home they are selling) to use to buy it, which will amount to roughly 10%. This guarantee will not only help you get more business (since you are eliminating risk that might otherwise hold a buyer back) but will also give you a great story to market.

11. If your clients are unsure about the loan process or what their payments will be for different programs, set up an in-person meeting with a great loan officer. Even if you are great with loans and numbers, a good loan officer will be able to help the buyer more than you can.

12. Use risk-mitigation strategies to help buyers improve offers, if needed. One way to do this is to tell them in advance you will use part of your commission to cover a portion of a low appraisal, if

needed. For example, if buyers are nervous about waving an appraisal, but you feel it might be necessary to win the offer, you might want to consider telling them you will cover a certain amount. Study the comparables and make sure you are confident the home will appraise. This is an especially good idea if the home is one that does not come up for sale a lot, and if missing out now might require much more time on everyone's part waiting for the next one to come up for sale. The home most likely will appraise, and you will get the full value of the deal. If it does not, and you have to give up part of your commission, do not worry. Eighty percent of something is better than 100% of nothing, and you will have a very good marketing story as well as clients who will refer more business to you.

13. If you have clients looking for a hard-to-find home, look everywhere you can to find it. I once helped a client buy a townhome by finding a listing agent's "Coming Soon!" ad on Craigslist. They were able to purchase the home before it went on the market and avoid what would have been a bidding war.

14. Get creative when dealing with builders. If the home is in the planning or earlier stages of building, it might still be possible to take out features the buyers do not want (reduces costs) and add in other features they do want (increases costs).

15. When it comes to home inspection repairs, many time sellers do not want to deal with the hassle of making repairs and/or scheduling work. You might be able to bring more value to your buyers by negotiating for a credit.

16. If you hear that a home is coming on the market and you have an interested buyer, do not be afraid to put a note under the door telling the sellers that you have an interested buyer. This can work even if someone else has the listing. I did this for one of my buyer clients, and the seller's agent contacted me saying the owner had gotten the note. I asked if they would be interested in possibly selling the home prior to going on the market. They were, and my clients were able to buy the home and avoid what probably would have been a bidding war.

17. Many times, builders will offer incentives if your buyers use their designated lender. These often make a lot of sense, but make sure you shop the lenders. Getting quotes from other lenders will often make the builder's designated lenders drop their rates, and you still get to keep the incentives for your buyers. This is an easy but great way to add value.

18. If you have clients looking for new-construction homes, make sure you let builders and/or their representatives know that you have a presence in their area and might have other buyers looking for their homes. This will help you negotiate the best possible deal for your buyer because you will be seen as someone who has a better chance of bringing several clients.

19. At open houses, a great way to show value quickly to buyers is to mention other homes you know about that are coming up for sale but are not on the market yet. This tells them that you can offer them something they cannot find on their own and something that other people cannot offer them.

20. Look to other industries for better ways to do business. If you do something in your industry that everyone is doing and do it better than others, you will add a little bit of value and therefore make a little money. If you do something in your industry that no one is doing, you will add a lot of value and therefore make a lot of money.

LEAD GENERATION

21. Buyer seminars are a great way to meet buyers in your target area. Pick a popular restaurant in the area or a meeting space in a condo or clubhouse in a neighborhood in your target area. Partner with a lender and title company so that you have more marketing resources. Create reasons for people to come, such as raffling off prizes and offering guarantees to buyers who attend and then use you. (I offer a guarantee to buyers at my seminars that I will be able to negotiate at least 3% off the list price or I will pay them the difference in cash).

22. Facebook advertisements are a great low-cost way to reach your target audience. Since Facebook has a lot of data on its users, you can target your advertisements in several different ways. The advertisements can be used both for raising brand awareness and getting users to take action. Make sure the landing page you send them to has compelling and relevant information and a strong call to action.

23. Get lots of directional signs that are branded with you or your team. At a minimum you should have three different types of directional signs: Coming Soon, for sale, and open house. Everyone on your team should use them. If you do not have time and are having someone else from your brokerage hold one of your listings' open houses, give that agent your directional sign to use.

24. Look for ways to find out which people in your target area are planning to move. One way to do this is to establish relationships with people who routinely find out about people's plans to move. Some examples are concierge staff in condo buildings, CPAs and financial planners, attorneys, and HR directors.

25. When you help buyers get a home off-market, make sure you negotiate with the sellers so that you can have your sign on their home and to market the home as being sold by you. Make sure you tell the buyer your plans for doing this and explain to them that the sign arrangement in no way affects your representation of them.

26. If you sell a home off-market in your target area, make sure you market that fact early and often. You want to communicate to prospects in your target area that you can get them a quick and hassle-free sale and that you have buyers looking in their area.

27. If you get a sale on a type of property that has not turned over in the last several months or years, chances are you are going to sell it for one of the highest prices ever. If that is the case, make sure you market that achievement to your target area.

28. Use tax records to create a mailing list in your target area. Make sure you send mail to them on a consistent basis.

29. Use upcoming listings to get more buyer clients. When you are able to tell a potential buyer about upcoming listings you have, you are creating and showing them value. If they see that working with you will get them access to listings that are not on the market, you are giving them something they will not get from all agents.

30. If you receive multiple offers on a listing, make sure you communicate that to people who own similar types of listings. If one of the buyers loses out, chances are good that they would make an offer on a similar place. For example, if I sold a one-bedroom condo in a building and had multiple offers, I would place notes under every other one-bedroom condo in the building telling them that a buyer just missed out on a home like theirs.

31. If you have a great lender and are expecting to have a busy open house, invite him or her to it. He or she can help with traffic flow, information capture, establishing rapport, educating buyers on loan programs, and even qualifying motivated prospects.

32. Ads can generally be one of two types with respect to focus: shotgun or rifle shots. The shotgun ad is wide and uses broad descriptive terms. Think of it as a funnel. These ads are designed to attract a wide variety of people, regardless of price point, the exact location, or other features of the home. In this type of ad you will not mention the exact price, location, or specifics about other features. You want lots of leads coming. When they call, you will find out their exact criteria and sort them accordingly. In contrast, the rifle ad is designed to attract a buyer who wants the particular house being advertised. It should be very detailed and descriptive. Both types of ads have a place in your business.

33. Use "Coming Soon!" signs and similar types of advertising in direct mail, online, and e-mails to market your listings before they go on the market.

34. Make sure you use several branded directional signs for your open houses. Add balloons to them to make them stand out. Use multiple signs at high-traffic intersections.

35. At open houses, try to sell the home you are showing first, but do not overdo it. If buyers do not want the house, being too pushy will only make them dig their heels in and resist. Mention other houses in the area that are on the market, or better yet, ones you know of that are coming up for sale but are not on the market yet. This approach has several benefits. It will make the prospective buyers more likely to trust you. It will show them your value in finding homes that might better meet their needs. It will also make them more likely to like the house you are in because they will sense you are not pushing it on them.

36. In a market with very low inventory or when you get a listing that is very unique, do an open house the evening of the first day it comes on the market, usually a Thursday. You can even market it as a wine-and-cheese event. This is a great way to get the most motivated buyers (they are the ones who will see it on short notice) all in the home at the same time to create a sense of urgency and fear of loss.

37. If you hear that a home is coming on the market and you have an interested buyer, do not be afraid to put a note under the door telling the sellers that you have an interested buyer. This can work even if someone else has the listing. I did this for one of my buyer clients, and the seller's agent contacted me saying the owner had gotten the note. I asked if they would be interested in possibly selling the home prior to going on the market. They were, and my clients were able to buy the home and avoid what probably would have been a bidding war.

BULLSEYE TARGETING

38. If you hear that someone may be moving, go after the business, especially if it is in your target area. One of my favorite techniques

was to put a letter under their door stating that I had a client look-ing for a home just like theirs and that if they were thinking about moving I might be able to help them get a great offer without even going on the market.

39. If you are working with buyers who cannot find anything they like on the market, find what they need before it comes on the market. Use tax records and past sales to analyze what types of homes would work for them. Make a list. Write compelling handwritten notes stating that you have a client ready to buy their home and they can avoid the hassle and costs of putting their home on the market. Place them on or under the doors of the target list in un-marked envelopes.

PRICING HOMES

40. If the inventory and turnover are low, get creative about how you analyze price. If it has been several months or years since the last sale of a particular type of home, you might have to use a parallel analysis where you compare other types of home sales over that time period and get a general rate of return, and then apply that to the subject home.

41. If you have a unique listing to sell and there has been no turnover of that type of unit, use parallel analysis to help develop your sales price. Look at comparables that have turned over in the time pe-riod since the last sale of the unique home and then apply that same rate of price growth to get an estimate of price

42. Know when to set a high anchor price. If you are pricing a home for sellers and it is very unique or one where there has not been a lot of turnover, it might make sense to use a higher list price to set the anchor price high. If there is uncertainty about the price be-cause of low turnover, there will also be uncertainty about when the next time a home like that will become available. That fear of loss might be enough if the right buyers come along.

43. Know when to set a price low enough to create a bidding war. Sometimes slightly underpricing a home can drive a lot of traffic

to a listing and create urgency and fear of loss and thereby result in a bidding war that will get the sellers more money than they expected.

WORKING WITH BUYERS

44. Always analyze the different costs with different types of homes when showing them. Condos tend to have the highest fees, followed by townhomes and then single-family homes. The difference in these fees can easily be equivalent to $100,000 in mortgages and sometimes as much as $200,000 or more. For example, a buyer looking for a two-bedroom condo that costs $500,000 and has a $500 monthly condo fee could actually save money by getting a townhome for $600,000 that only has a $50 monthly HOA fee.

45. If a buyer client loses out on a home, either because they did not move fast enough or they did not write a strong enough offer, use it as a chance to establish the point that they will be in a better position now to act when the right home comes up.

46. When working with move-up buyers review their options and establish timelines up front. Make sure you have them talk to a qualified lender up front and determine if they need to sell their home first before buying the next one.

47. Make sure you do a reality check analysis for your buyers at the beginning of the process. This is basically a search where you take their criteria (location, features, size, price point) and do a backward search to find out what has sold in the past 12 months. This search lets them know if their expectations are realistic and if they need to adjust any of their criteria. It will also give them a good idea of the turnover rate, which will help them determine how selective or flexible they can be when a target home becomes available.

48. If buyers lose out on a place, make sure you show them other places soon, so that they don't lose momentum. A bonus is when you can show them places off-market.

49. During negotiations, do not be afraid to ask for more than your clients are expecting. The worse case is you will leave more room to get what they are looking for, and the best case is you will get them more than they thought they could.

50. If a negotiation failed at first and the home is still on the market a week or more later, do not be afraid to reengage the seller and/or listing agent. Sometimes time is all it takes for both sides to be willing to give more.

51. If you ever hear buyers saying they could get a better deal by going directly to a new-construction representative, remind them that they might represent one deal to the builder but a good agent can represent several potential deals. Who do you think the builder sales rep will give a better deal to—the person representing one deal or the listing agent who can bring several potential buyers?

WORKING WITH SELLERS

52. Before you meet with sellers, pre-sell them on your value. Send them a pre-listing packet that tells them about you and your team and about how you will provide more value than anyone else. Make sure you include statistical proof and testimonials from previous clients.

53. If sellers do not need to sell their home right away, the time to start marketing their home is now. After they sign a listing agreement, begin marketing their home. Use your website, social media, direct mail, signs, and direct e-mail. Doing this provides value to them because it helps develop interest in their home before it goes on the MLS, and it provides value to you because it will help you find more buyers.

Appendix

54. If buyers use a lender you are not familiar with and you are unsure about that lender's ability to close, ask them to make a backup application with a lender who you know will be able to close. It is better to have the backup and not need it than to need it and not have it.

55. In a multiple-offer situation, remember that this is a business, and your job when representing sellers is to get them the best possible offer in terms of both price and terms.

56. In a multiple-offer situation, it usually makes sense to give potential buyers the chance to resubmit offers or ask them to submit their highest and best offer. Remember that a deal is not done until both the buyers and the sellers have signed off and delivered the contract to the other party.

57. Make the job of the appraisers as easy as possible. Meet them face-to-face at the home or have someone from your team meet them. Provide them with a packet that shows the comparable sold homes that justify your price. This information may or may not make their job easier, but at the very least it will help appraisers put a face to the job and make them less likely to pick your home out of huge pile they are working on as the one to give a low appraisal to.

58. If you are representing sellers and get a low appraisal, do not assume you have to automatically lower the price if the buyers had an appraisal contingency. Try other options such as challenging the appraisal, requesting a new lender, and negotiating with the buyers to cover some or all of the difference. Every situation has its own circumstances, but you must always try to create the most value in every case.

59. If you are competing against one or more established agents with long track records and you are new to the industry or area, remember this: If established agents make a mistake on a listing, they still have a long track record to fall back on, but if newcomers make mistakes, that might eliminate their chance to get business in that area for a long time. There is definitely an argument that since newer agents have more to lose, they might do a better job than an

experienced agent. Make sure you understand that and make this case if you are competing for a listing against an established agent.

60. If you are competing against other agents for listings, make sure that you research their statistics. At a minimum, look at their total volume, volume in that area, average days on market, list price to sold price ratio, and their total percentage withdrawal/expired listings. If you have a statistical advantage in these areas, the prospective sellers deserve to know.

61. If you or other agents have buyers interested in a home before it goes on the market, schedule the pre-market showings back-to-back or at the same time. This will help create the fear of loss and urgency to write an offer in the buyers.

62. In a market with very low inventory or when you get a listing that is very unique, do an open house the evening of the first day it comes on the market, usually a Thursday. You can even market it as a wine-and-cheese event. This is a great way to get the most motivated buyers (they are the ones who will see it on short notice) all in the home at the same time to create a sense of urgency and fear of loss.

63. When you sign a new listing, communicate this to all of the buyers and prospects you are working with who might be interested in that home. Communicate it to agents in your office and brokerage as well.

64. When it comes to signs and homeowner association regulations, it is better to ask for forgiveness than permission. Getting your signs up drives traffic to your listing, which helps your sellers get the best price possible. It also helps establish your presence in the area.

65. Understand that more often than not, but not always, the first offer sellers get is going to be the best one. Make sure you let them know this, especially if they feel insulted about an offer. The process itself can be very emotional for sellers, so many times you have a difficult job of bringing a steady, rational approach to the situation while still empathizing with them.

GETTING A DEAL DONE

66. Know when to cut a commission to get a listing. If you are well established and have a track record of success in a certain target area, you should not have to reduce your commission. If you are starting out and breaking into a new area, reducing your commission might be needed to gain market share. Make sure when you do it that you get the sellers' commitment to sign right away and that you get their commitment to refer more business to you.

67. Know when to give a buyer rebate or cut a commission in order to help get a deal done. If it is a deal that will help you gain initial market share or give you a good marketing opportunity, then you should lean toward cutting your commission. If there is no other likely sale that will happen if the deal does not get done, then you should also lean toward cutting. When you do cut your commission, make sure you tell the clients you are doing it because you expect great testimonials and referrals from them, and be sure to get their commitment to do so.

68. Practice future pacing both when buyers are close to the offer stage and after they go under contract. Future pacing in this regard is telling them about all the great ways in which they will use and enjoy the home in the future. A few examples would be how they will enjoy walking to all the nearby restaurants, how they will enjoy entertaining in the great room, how the dining room will be big enough for meals when their children and children's spouses visit, or how their young children will enjoy the backyard.

69. If you are in a tough negotiation and the buyers and sellers cannot come to terms, remember that there are more than two sources of money in a deal. In addition to the buyers and sellers, the buyers' agent, sellers' agent, lenders, and title companies can all give money to help make a deal happen. Look for as many people as possible who can help make a deal happen.

70. Make sure you tout the strength of your lender to the sellers or listing agent when presenting your offer, especially if it is going to be a competitive situation or the buyers are trying to close quickly.

71. If buyers are interested in a house that has just come on the market, and the listing agent wants to hold an open house or wait to review offers, ask what kind of offer it would take for the sellers to feel good about selling it now. Many times they will give the price and terms and let your buyers take it off the market before more people see it.

72. If you are working with investors looking to purchase a rental property, one way you can help win their business or get a tough deal done is to offer to help them find the first renter at a discounted rate.

73. If your buyers are looking at new homes, remember that the builders or developers are usually more likely to negotiate on items that do not show up in the sales price. Some examples are giving closing-cost credits, giving upgrades, and paying for condo fees or HOA dues. This is a great way to create tons of value for your buyers and get them the best possible deal.

74. Make sure you sell the strength of your buyers' lender to the listing agent or seller, especially in a competing situation. Have the lender call the listing agent and/or present a list of loans in the area that the lender has closed.

75. If you are going to be in a potential multiple-offer situation and the listing agent or sellers will not review offers before a certain deadline, ask how many other offers they have and what kind of terms it will take to win. You might not get a direct answer, but their reaction might help you get a feel for what is needed.

76. In a competing situation, ask the listing agent or sellers if a price of "x" would be good enough to win. Again, you might not get a direct answer, but their reaction might help you determine what is needed.

77. In a multiple-offer situation, where there is a deadline and no chance that the sellers will review offers ahead of time, have your offer ready but do not submit it until shortly before the deadline. You do not want your offer to be used as leverage to shop for better ones.

78. If you have a track record of closings in an area, make sure you let the listing agent know in competing situations. It makes your clients' case better.

79. If your clients are in a competitive offer situation and want to include an appraisal contingency, see if they are willing to shorten the time period to less than the "standard" time.

80. If your clients are in a competitive situation and want to include the appraisal contingency, see if they are willing to cover a certain amount in the event of a low appraisal. For example, if the price is $500,000, maybe they are willing to cover the first $10,000 of a low appraisal. This gives them protection if the appraisal comes in really low but makes their offer look better than that of a buyer with a regular appraisal contingency.

81. If your clients are in a competitive situation and want to include a home inspection contingency, see if they are willing to make the time period shorter than the "standard" time period.

82. If your clients are in a competitive situation and want to include a home inspection contingency, see if they are willing to make the contingency for informational purposes only. This tells the sellers that the buyers are not going to nickel-and-dime them but gives your clients protection in case something is terribly wrong with the house.

Reviews and Referrals

83. The best time to ask for a review or for a referral is at the time of sale. This is when your clients' excitement and interest is usually at the highest. Let them know how important reviews and referrals are and that those two things are a sign from them that your service was exceptional, and that if they do not feel liked doing this for you, then you will interpret that as a sign that you failed them.

84. When you help buyers get a home before it is on the market (or if you negotiate a good deal on a home that is on the market), reaffirm to them frequently throughout the process how great a deal

they got. This will help them avoid any potential buyer's remorse. It will also help them see more of the value that you provided and get you more referrals.

85. If you do a great job for sellers, get them to give you social proof — a written recommendation, online review, video testimonial, or all three.

86. If you get a lead or referral from someone, whether it be a client, friend, doorman at a condo building, or another individual, make sure you reward that person at the time of the referral. You should also reward them again at the time of closing, but it is important to reward the initial referral, which is the behavior you want repeated.

87. No matter what segment you pick for your target segment, treat your current and past clients like another target segment. Mail to them, give them gifts throughout the year, call them, and invite them to client events. If you stay in a good relationship with them, they will use you again and refer more clients to you.

New Clients

88. At your initial contact with potential buyers and sellers, you must establish timing and motivation. If you do not know why the clients want to take action and when they want to take action, you will not be in a position to know how to create the most value for them.

89. When scheduling a listing appointment, try to find out in advance if the sellers are talking to other agents. The majority of the time they will not be doing so, but when they are, it helps to know to whom they are talking ahead of time so you can research the best way to position yourself as the agent who can create the most value for them.

90. If sellers are going to interview more than one agent, it is best if you can schedule yourself to go last. Make sure you tell the sellers about the preparation you will do for the meeting and get their commitment not to sign with anyone before meeting with you. It

helps to go last because you are then in the best position to show them how you will create the most value, because after talking with the other agents, they will have reference points.

91. If you cannot schedule yourself to be the last listing agent to meet with sellers, your goal for the meeting should be one of two outcomes. Ideally, get them to commit to using you and cancel the other meetings. If you are going to provide the most value and do the best job, you are saving everyone's time by doing this. If they are not ready to commit, get them to commit to meeting or talking with you after they have met with everyone but before they have made their decision.

92. Try to avoid the price and commission conversation with sellers before they commit to using you. If sellers do not think you are the best person to sell their home, then what does your opinion about value mean to them anyway. Too often sellers will go with the person who either tells them the highest price their home will sell for or offers the lowest commission. Listing at a higher price (especially if it is too high) and hiring the cheapest person who will do the job are rarely the best methods for sellers to net the most amount of money.

93. Talk to your buyers about the other considerations in an offer (contingencies, type of financing, down payment, closing time, etc.) early in the process. You want them to be able to think through all of these items well in advance of when they have to make an actual decision.

94. Don't ever give up when you are competing for a listing, especially if it is in your target area. If you are establishing a foothold in the area, you might have to make a serious cut in your rate to beat out an agent who is already established in the area. Know what your true costs are in servicing the listing in terms of both time and money. Also, understand your true upside in getting the listing (exposure in the target market, meeting new buyers, potential future business, etc.). Only then will you know at what rate you can logically take the listing.

95. If you come in contact with potential sellers, and they are not ready to list and are considering interviewing other agents, bring interested buyers by their home if they agree to pay you a buyer agent fee. If they see you bringing buyers to their home without even having it listed, it will help you earn the listing when they do decide to list.

96. When competing for a listing, ask other agents in your office if they have buyers interested in it. If you are able to bring those buyers to view the home prior to getting the listing, it will show the sellers you have the ability to find them buyers.

97. At open houses, try to sell the home you are showing first, but do not overdo it. If buyers do not want the house, being too pushy will only make them dig their heels in and resist. Mention other houses in the area that are on the market, or better yet, ones you know of that are coming up for sale but are not on the market yet. This approach has several benefits. It will make the prospective buyers more likely to trust you. It will show them your value in finding homes that might better meet their needs. It will also make them more likely to like the house you are in because they will sense you are not pushing it on them.

98. Make sure you get buyers to sign in at open houses and at a minimum get their name, phone number, and e-mail address. Fill out a few cards with names and the information you want so people arriving will think people before them gave the information. It will make them more likely to sign in because they will think others did so too.

99. Don't lose out on potential clients just because they have relocation benefits with a certain brokerage. Most of the time all it takes to become "relocation qualified" is to sign a referral agreement with the relocation company.

100. Don't be afraid of For Sale By Owner prospects (FSBOs). Many times they will agree to pay you a buyer agent fee for bringing them a buyer. The more buyers you can bring them, the more likely they will be to list with you when they decide to hire an agent and really try to sell their home.

Index

A

Accountant, 116
Adjustable Rate Mortgages, 41
Adjustable Rate Mortgages (ARMs), 41
Adwords, 89
American Planning Association, 8
Anchor Price, 165
Appraisals, 57, 74, 86
Appraisers, 33, 54, 55, 56, 86, 168
ARMs, 41
Association Dues, 2
Attorneys, 8, 162
Audit, 116

B

Bidding War, 165
Bidding Wars, 100, 101, 151
Brand Awareness, 162
Broker Agreement, 45, 139
Broker Fees, 2
Builders, 120, 121, 151, 160, 161, 171
Buyer Agreement, 62, 68
Buyer Clients, 11, 16, 160, 163, 164
Buyer Leads, 77, 133, 155

C

Call To Action, 162
Capital Gains Tax, 98
Cash Flow Positive Home, 135
Cash-To-Close, 53
Century 21, 4
Classic Homes, 120, 121, 122
Client Testimonials, Iv
Closing Costs For The Buyer, 53
Closings Costs, 53, 121
Commission Reduction, 16
Commissions, 67, 137
Comparable Sales, 18, 103, 139
Comparables, Viii, 56, 71, 72, 76, 77, 86, 87, 99, 107, 122, 160, 165
Competing For A Listing, 175
Competing-Offer, 34
Competitive Interest Rates, 61
Conventional Loans, 61

Costs Paid By The Seller, 53
CPAs, 8, 162
Craigslist, 20, 36, 38, 67, 75, 83, 125, 127, 135, 158, 160
Credit Scores, 61

D

Defense Contractor, I, 1, 76
Demographics, 149
Designated Lender, 161
Direct Mail, 11, 27, 38, 51, 80, 82, 94, 113, 118, 125, 132, 136, 151, 157, 163, 167
Distribution Channels, 38
Down Payment, 46, 47, 52, 61, 63, 111, 114, 115, 116, 117, 123, 128, 174

E

Earnest Money, 57, 114
E-Mail Lists, 158
Escalation Clause, 73, 103
Established Agents, 7, 168
Expenses, 2, 4, 115, 134, 135, 136

F

Facebook, 38, 80, 84, 153, 162
Facebook Advertisements, 162
FHA, 57, 61, 66, 119, 123
Financial Planners, 162
Financing Approval, 54, 58
For Sale By Owner Prospects (FSBOs), 175
FSBO, 14, 21, 22, 127
Funnel, 4, 133, 163
Funnel Leads, 4

G

Google, 89, 94

H

Handwritten Note, 13, 141
Hiring Agents, 9
HOA, 12, 128, 166, 171
Home Inspection, 20, 32, 33, 34, 35, 46, 53, 54, 55, 72, 73, 74, 85, 87, 98, 103, 128, 131, 142, 160, 172
Home Inspectors, 34
Home Values, 120

I

Incentives, 65, 161

K

Keri Shull Team, I, 16, 9, 155

L

Lead Generation, 24, 71
Lead Generation, 161
Licensing And Education, 2

List Price, 15
Loan Officers, 97
Loan Program, 2, 29, 62, 66, 159
Lockbox Fees, 2
Long-Term Success, 17, 5

M

Mailing List, 163
Make Me Move (MMM), 22
Marketing Budget, 7, 150
Marketing Expenses, 2
Marketing Materials, Iv, 118
Marketing Strategy, Iv, 79, 89, 90, 104, 121, 127
MBA Graduates, 1
Metro System, 7
MLS, 20, 27, 38, 57, 58, 82, 91, 101, 119, 122, 127, 128, 144, 167
Mortgage Insurance Payment, 61
Move-Up Buyers, 8, 137, 159, 166
Multiple Listing Fees, 2
Multiple Offers, 30, 48, 102, 113, 163
Multiple-Offer, 168, 171

N

National Association Of Realtors, 2
Naval Academy, I, 1
Negotiate A Good Deal, 172
Negotiating Strategy, Iv
New Clients, 173
New Construction, 144
Newsletters, 26, 27, 38, 106, 118
No Money Down, 135
Non-Contingent, 58

O

Off-Market, 76, 162, 167
Off-Market Showings, 76
Online Ads, 38
Online Review, 173
Open House, Iv, V, 15, 18, 35, 38, 39, 43, 54, 57, 58, 71, 72, 83, 84, 85, 89, 96, 97, 98, 99, 101, 102, 104, 108, 109, 110, 113, 114, 118, 122, 127, 129, 130, 138, 162, 163, 164, 169, 171
Open House Showings, V
Open Houses Is With Crowd Control, 39
Optime Realty, 3, I, 5, 155

P

Parallel Analysis, 105, 107, 165
Poverty Level, 2
Pre-Approval, 68, 73, 111, 130, 139
Pre-Listing Packet, 118, 119, 125, 167

Pre-Market Campaign, 35, 36, 96
Pre-Market Showings, 83, 169
Pre-Selling, 118
Price Adjustments, 45
Price Point, 149
Price Reduction, 110
Pricing Homes, 165
Private Mortgage Insurance (PMI), 123
Private Showings, 75, 76, 97
Profit And Loss, 116
Pulte, 148
Purpose Of Staging, 36

R

Real Estate License, 2, 3, 7
REALTOR®, 2
Redfin, 4, 141
Redwood Realty Office, 4
Regulations, 58, 169
Renovations, 62, 63, 102, 120
Rent-Back, 100, 128
Requests For Showings, 53
Résumé, 76
Reviews And Referrals, 172

S

Scheduling A Listing Appointment, 173
Scheduling Showings, 90
Segment The Market, 7, 150, 157
Segment Your Market, 149
Self-Employment Taxes, 2
Seller Credit, 117
Seller Financing, 133, 135
Seller's Agent, 160, 164
Signs
    Coming Soon, For Sale, And Open House, 162
Social Media, 24, 27, 38, 51, 77, 80, 82, 83, 85, 94, 98, 109, 151, 157, 167
Social Proof, 50, 173
Staging A Property, 35

T

Target Segment, 157, 158, 173
Target Your Advertisements, 162
Tax Records, 22, 140, 146, 163, 165
Tenants In Place, 135
Testimonials And Referrals, 170
The STP Framework, 7
Track Record Of Success, 66, 77, 100, 158, 170
Track Records, 39, 168
Transaction Costs, 16

Transactions, 3, 6, 10, 65, 80, 114, 150, 154, 155
Trulia, 20, 36
Turnover Rate, 150, 166
Twitter, 38, 153

U

Under Contract, 125
Underwriting, 33, 35, 54, 66
Unique Home, 165
Unique Value Proposition, 9
USAA, 43, 74

V

Vehicle Expenses, 2
Video Testimonial, 173
Virtual Tours, 38
Virtual Video Tours, 38

W

Walk-Through, 20, 131
Website, 10, 11, 29, 36, 38, 79, 118, 157, 167

Y

Youtube, 38, 80, 109, 118, 121

Z

Zero Down, 135
Zillow, 20, 22, 36, 127

Join Our Team

We always have room on our team for top-talent individuals!

At The Keri Shull and Orange Line Living Team, you'll learn from the best in the business and receive hands-on real estate training that will teach you to make more money in less time.

Unlike other brokerages, the agents on our team average 24 transactions a year. We have top-quality transaction and back-end support that allows you to devote your time and energy to your clients.

If you're ready to start building the real estate career of your dreams, it's time for you to join the best team.

You have a goal – we have the business model and expertise to make it happen.

Give us a call, shoot us an email, or visit the link below to get in touch.

(703) 589-9057
recruiting@kerishullteam.com
HyperFastCareers.com

Learn About Coaching

Tired of working 50+ hours a week and not making any money? Do you want to make more money in less time and strike a better work-life balance?

Join the HyperFast Agent Inner Circle to learn how to generate quality, low-cost leads. The Inner Circle is full of specialized training on how to make more money in real estate.

Inner Circle members receive exclusive access to the strategies and re-sources our team uses to boost sales and outperform all of our com-petitors. Our coaching, downloadable reports, and weekly calls will give you the tools to master all areas of real estate including:

Database Management:
Learn how to leverage your database to convert leads you already have into clients, referrals, and repeat business.

Recruiting:
Looking to expand? Learn the best recruiting practices from a team of over 60 people! We teach you how to stop wasting your time and re-sources hiring the wrong people.

Sales Conversion:
Learn how to convert leads on the phone, then implement follow-up strategies to convert longer-term leads.

Just for readers of this book, we're offering a **30-day trial of the HyperFast Inner Circle for just $1**!

Visit HyperFastTrial.com for more information, or contact:

(703) 436-6994
info@HyperFastAgent.com

Referral Network for Agents

Start getting referrals in your location today!

There is no easier way to increase sales in your market than to become one of our referral affiliates.

Referrals are the easiest way for you to generate extra income. We have a huge team and a massive network, and there's a good chance that we know people moving to your area.

Grow your sales, visibility, and network by partnering with The Keri Shull Team. Give us a call, shoot us an email, or visit the link below to get in touch.

(703) 589-9057
info@HyperFastAgent.com

Looking to Buy or Sell?

Buyers - We want you to love your new home!
That is why if your home isn't a perfect fit for you, we will buy it back!
When you work with us, you will be the first to receive access to listings that match your criteria, before other buyers, so you can avoid
viewing homes that don't meet your needs and negotiate the lowest
possible price for the home you like most.

Sellers - We sell homes for more money in less time!
If you're not satisfied with the new purchase of your home, we will
buy it back, or sell it for free — guaranteed!

Many agents offer these kinds of guarantees as a bait-and-switch to
get new business — not us. Keri and I have spent over $12 million
backing up our guarantee, because we know we have what it takes to
sell your home at the right price.

Give us a call, shoot us an email, or visit the link below to get in touch.

(703) 589-9057
contact@kerishullteam.com
kerishull.com